D1384919

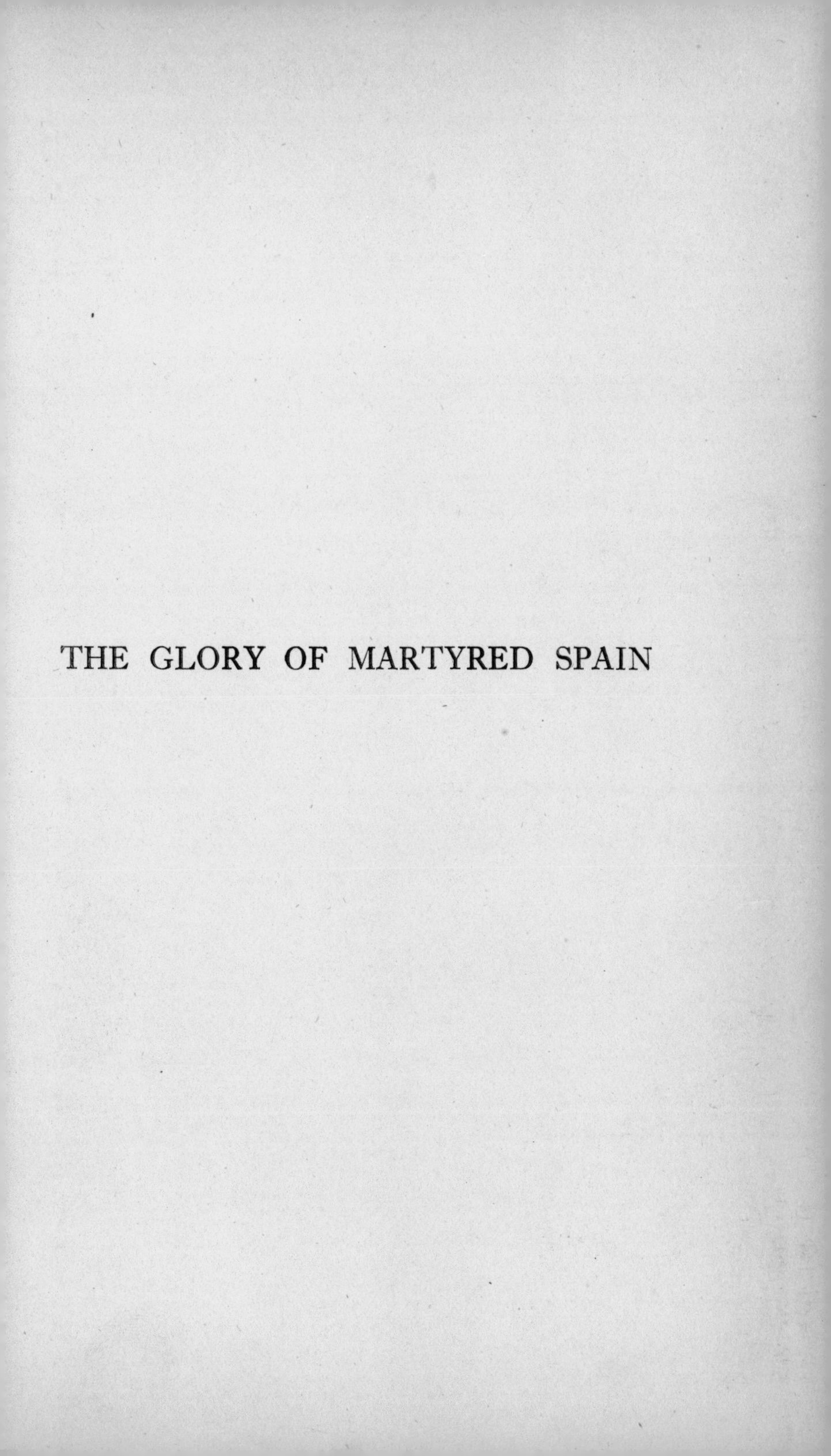

THE GLORY OF MARTYRED SPAIN

THE GLORY OF MARTYRED SPAIN

NOTES ON THE RELIGIOUS PERSECUTION

By

LUIS CARRERAS

TRANSLATED FROM THE SPANISH

LONDON

BURNS OATES & WASHBOURNE LTD

PUBLISHERS TO THE HOLY SEE

NIHIL OBSTAT:

JOANNES V. SIMCOX, D.C.L.,
Censor deputatus.

IMPRIMATUR:

LEONELLUS CAN. EVANS,
Vic. Gen.

WESTMONASTERII,
die 7a Martii 1939.

MADE AND PRINTED IN GREAT BRITAIN
FOR
BURNS OATES & WASHBOURNE LTD
1939

CONTENTS

PART I

ORIGINS OF THE RELIGIOUS PERSECUTION

PART II

FLOS MARTYRUM

PART I

ORIGINS OF THE RELIGIOUS PERSECUTION

CHAPTER I

THE ACCUSATION

ONE of the most infamous accusations made against the Church by a certain type of international propagandist, as well as by semi-Catholic opponents of Fascism, was that the rising of July 18, 1936 was brought about jointly by the Church and the Army, and that the Church is therefore immediately and directly responsible for its partial extermination under the Proletarian Revolution. This accusation began to be spread abroad at the same time as the churches began to be fired and priests to be murdered.

Our first task is to examine the evidence adduced in support of that accusation.

Soon after the Pope had delivered his moving allocution to the Spanish refugees in Rome, an anti-clerical ex-Minister of the Republic, Don Marcelino Domingo, saw fit to make the following reply :

> " Obstinately pursuing her attitude of belligerency, after her defeat at the polls, the Church prepared to gain her victory by force of arms. Bishops and Generals set to work together, and in this collusion organized the insurrection. . . . Is Pius XI aware of the identity of the leader of the revolution in Burgos ? It was the Archbishop. Does Pius XI know why Segovia, on the point of capitulating, resolved in the end to continue the struggle ? Because of the vote of the Bishop."[1]

Since the very beginning of the War there has been a little group of dissentient Catholics eager to seize every opportunity of attacking the Church. In the sacred name of religion, and under the pretence of serving its deepest and

[1] *L'Œuvre,* September 17, 30, 1936. (Cf. Jean-Richard Bloch : *Espagne, Espagne !* pp. 224–35.) On September 23 the *Osservatore Romano* published a vigorous and detailed reply.

truest interests, they have been aiding the anti-God revolution with so-called Catholic propaganda, which begins by attempting to whitewash the Republic's policy of persecution, goes on to attack the Spanish hierarchy, repeats the legend that the Church was the aggressor of the " people " and the responsible author of the rebellion, and finally affirms that a victory for the Reds would in a true and practical sense promote the Christian religion.

> " Because I am a Catholic and defend freedom of conscience ", declared Señor Ossorio y Gallardo, the Red Spanish Ambassador in Paris and Brussels, " and because I know that the Republicans are defending justice, freedom and faith, I give my support to the Republicans, and, together with many other Catholics, am anxious to defend Spain against Fascism."[1]

Don José Bergamín, editor of the intellectualist review *Cruz y Raya*, goes so far as to define Catholicism in the following terms :

> " For a long time our clergy had ceased to serve God. . . . The Spanish Church had accumulated tremendous riches and had become one of the most terrible oppressors of the workers. . . . For years, in *Cruz y Raya*, I have been combating the impiety of official religion and I was glad to join the Association of Revolutionary Writers, in which are to be found the foremost representatives of Spanish letters. In Spain the victory of the people will mean the triumph of the true Christian faith " (*Vu*, p. 54).

This " Group of the Nine Spanish Catholics ", as it is sometimes ironically termed, consists of four well-known priests, two Red ambassadors and three self-styled Catholic writers. A manifesto which it published on the War and the Madrid bombardments was used as an authoritative source, in a way which its authors might perhaps not have wished, by pamphlets disseminated in various countries and containing outrageous and calumnious propaganda on the causes

[1] Señor Ossorio y Gallardo also states (*La Dépêche*, December 24, 1936) that the principal Catholic review in Spain is on the side of the Government.

and nature of the Spanish War, put together with a view to influencing Catholic opinion abroad. Here are some extracts from the pamphlet which circulated in Switzerland.

> "Before the battle of Irún, the Bishop of Pamplona delivered a speech encouraging the rebels to make a 'decisive attack', and promised them as a reward a Mass in the Cathedral of Irún[1] when it should be conquered. The Bishop of Mondeno[2] led a column on Oviedo. At Pamplona, women who had been imprisoned, and whose husbands had been loyal defenders of the legitimate Government, were placed under the wardenship of nuns who inflicted mental tortures on them by telling them that their husbands had been shot and that they could thank God that they were not being shot too. In Pamplona, too, on the fifteenth of August, the Festival of the Assumption of Our Lady, the rebels heard Mass, after which eighty men were shot in groups of ten in the moats of the fortress."[3]

All kinds of other rumours went round. During the early days of the rising the news circulated in Barcelona that, among the leaders of the enemy's General Staff, observers in Government aeroplanes had recognized the Archbishop-Bishop of Majorca. When the expedition of the famous Captain Bayo was fighting in Majorca, in the middle of August, *La Vanguardia* declared that Bishop Miralles was making inspections of the front with the Staff, and was distributing ices to the soldiers from a lorry!

But this is comedy; and we must return to the main accusation against the Church—that its buildings were used as fortresses during the rebellion and that priests fired from them on the people.

Señor Marcelino Domingo formulates this accusation in what may be described as its "official" guise:

> "The Government notes that almost all the churches were turned into fortresses; that almost all the sacristies

[1] [There is no Cathedral in Irún.—Tr.]
[2] Presumably Mondoñedo.
[3] Josephe C. Bonnier: *Spanien: Ein Wort, katholische Männer und Frauen*, Zurich, 1937.

had become munition dumps and that the majority of the Bishops, priests and seminarists were *franc-tireurs* in the rebellion."

The following accusations were made by Don José M. de Semprún, whom Señor Ossorio y Gallardo, with no regard for terminological propriety, has described as a Catholic leader:

" Theoretically, it may be said that the adherence of a part—and a great part—of the clergy to the military revolt took place simultaneously with the attacks on persons and institutions connected with religion. But if we follow the actual historical order of events, it is certain that the measures taken by the Government with respect to religious institutions, including the acts of violence committed by more or less irresponsible left-wing elements, were *preceded* by the participation of the clergy, both regular and secular, in the revolt unleashed in the month of July. . . . They began by openly expressing their sympathy and moral support and finished by lending effective armed participation in the homicidal struggle."[1]

In the pamphlet just referred to, another author, Don Antonio Salcedo, whose evidence is supposed to have the greater value from his having written a book on St. Francis of Assisi, puts the following cynical questions :

" What churches have been destroyed ? Those from which the starving people were fired upon. What convents have been burned ? Those which were used as munition dumps."

Finally, Señor Ossorio y Gallardo, the notorious and voluble jurist and polemist who in the first months of the Republic described himself as a " Monarchist without a king ", delivered himself thus :

" It will be said that deeds of violence have been committed against the churches and the clergy. That is true. To deny it would be hypocrisy. But such deeds are only reprisals against those which the clergy had

[1] J. M. de Semprún : " La question d'Espagne inconnue," in *Esprit* November 1, 1936, pp. 291–319.

committed against the people. From the beginning of the War churches had been transformed into fortresses, from which the rebels had fired with rifles and machine-guns. . . .

"As a lawyer by profession, I am accustomed to give due weight to cause and consequence. And when I consider the conduct of certain Catholics and of the clergy of my country, I can only too well understand the reprisals taken by the masses, even while I deplore them."[1]

Supported as they were by persons calling themselves not only authorities on the political situation but also Catholics zealous of the Church's truest interests, is it surprising that the Popular Front and the Communist Press abroad should gleefully repeat these disgraceful accusations levelled against the Church's hierarchy?[2]

I doubt if there is a parallel to this for mental obliquity and for the loss of the sense of justice and humanity for which party passion has been responsible in the Spanish Civil War. Men still calling themselves Catholics, who have not written a word of condemnation on the mass assassinations of clergy and their flocks during the Revolution, maintain with cruel frigidity the guilt of the victims of these murders on evidence which they must know, or at least suspect, to be false.

But I doubt also if for pure dignity there is any parallel to the reply of the Spanish Bishops in their Joint Letter.[3]

[1] Speech of October 10, 1936. *La Dépêche*, Toulouse, December 24, 1936. *L'Avenir de l'Espagne*, February 22, 1937.

[2] Cf. the letter from the Communist Party of the northern region to Cardinal Liénart and the latter's reply and other correspondence reproduced in the *Osservatore Romano* of November 14, 1936.

It is surprising that in the camp most radically opposed to this there should be cases of animadversion against the Church, as in *Viva España! Arriba España!*, a book published by the anti-Bolshevik *Nibelungen* (Berlin, Leipzig, 1937) and written in German by a Dutch author, Maria de Smeth, who has paid long visits to Russia and claims to have spent six months in Nationalist Spain during the War. "Almost half the land of Spain," remarks this writer, "belongs to the Church and the convents, whence the quasi-paradoxical fury of the faithful in Spain against churches, convents, priests and nuns. . . . Certainly Moscow has selected the most appropriate country for its plans. In Spain we have the nearest approach to Tsarist Russia."

Elsewhere in this book (pp. 92, 102–4) the grossest insults are hurled at the clergy of Spain and Italy, and (pp. 205–6) at the Pope.

[3] *Joint Letter of the Spanish Bishops to the Bishops of the whole world concerning the War in Spain.* (London. Catholic Truth Society, 1937.)

Grieved though they are at the martyrdom of ten members of the Episcopate and of thousands of priests and religious, they recognize the affirmative value which their testimony will have throughout the world and confine themselves to saying :

> " The churches were burned because they were the Houses of God ; the clergy were sacrificed because they were the ministers of God. Proofs of this abound. The Church has not been an aggressor. She was the people's first benefactor, inculcating the doctrine of social justice and encouraging its works. She succumbed—where anarchical Communism prevailed—an innocent, peaceful and defenceless victim."[1]

The bitterest complaint of the Spanish Bishops is only this : " We have not even been done the honour of being considered as victims. Right and justice have been weighed in the same balance as wrong and injustice—the last perhaps the greatest that the centuries have seen."[2]

Infamy, no doubt, will pursue its way ; and this particular infamy has been accredited by a few foreign writers who look upon themselves as choice spirits, and who, without perhaps realizing the tainted nature of the sources from which they draw their material, attack what it would have been a most noble undertaking and a most Christian duty to defend.

[1] *Joint Letter*, p. 25. [2] *Joint Letter*, pp. 30–31.

CHAPTER II

PRELUDE TO THE PERSECUTION

ONLY foolishness or conscious deception could explain the attempts made to attribute to isolated incidents the persecution carried out during the Proletarian Revolution and beginning on July 19, 1936. It has only to be recalled that the vandalism of the Spanish revolutionaries began on May 11, 1931, barely a month after the proclamation of the Republic, and that, by the time that the war of liberation broke out five years later, incendiarism, organized by the revolutionaries and acquiesced in by the Government, had been responsible for the destruction of seven hundred churches and religious houses throughout Spain, over half of which had been destroyed during the brief five-months' reign of the Popular Front.

The origins and true causes of the persecution must be looked for elsewhere. Everyone knows that the dogmas of Marxism and the organizations responsible for the Anarcho-Communist revolution and the religious persecution which it brought in its train are inspired by a complete and radical atheism and aim at inaugurating an era of religious nihilism by means of destructive and iconoclastic "direct action," by comparison with which traditional anti-clericalism seems the merest ineffectual rhetoric.

The writings of Marx, Engels, Lenin, and Stalin were not only known in Spain, but had made a widespread and popular appeal to many among the masses.

The fundamental conception of religion held by Karl Marx took form as early as 1844 in his *Contribution to a criticism of the philosophy of Hegel.* "Religious misery," he said, "is on one hand the expression of real misery and on the other hand the protest against real misery. Religion is the sigh of the creature overwhelmed by unhappiness, of the soul in a heartless world ; and the spirit of a civilization from which the spirit is excluded. Religion is the opium of the people."[1]

Here we have the first explanation of the origins of religion which considers religion as a social phenomenon not dependent on the innate inclinations of the soul or on the evolutionary conditions of human society towards a higher existence, but as expressive of the worst degeneration of the race. Marx himself goes on to say that religion is an authentic product of capitalist society. " It is this social state and this society that produce religion, which is a state of world-conscience as absurd as the world that this state and society produce. . . . In this world religion is the general motive of consolation and justification." And Lenin goes still farther. " Economic slavery ", he says, " is the true cause of the brutifying of humanity by religion."

In a pamphlet entitled *On Religion*, Lenin published in collected form a series of articles which he had written between 1902 and 1920 ; in them he develops Marxist doctrine, carries it to its farthest conclusions and gives it an application of the most militant type.

According to Lenin, religion is an instrument for the exploitation of the proletariat by the *bourgeoisie*, the most direct expression of the " spiritual tyranny which everywhere and at all times weighs upon the masses of the people, already overwhelmed by perpetual labours for the advantages of others, by solitude and misery. . . . Religion is a crude form of spiritual alcohol, in which the slaves of Capital drown their human nature and the rights due to human nature for the sake of an existence which it is below man's dignity to lead " (p. 3).

Lenin then proceeds to expound his doctrine of " war upon religion ", and to detail the means by which he proposes to carry on this war :

> " The sensible worker of our time . . . is full of contempt for religious prejudices, leaves Heaven to *curas* and *bourgeois* hypocrites and sets out to gain for himself a better time in this world. The proletariat of to-day

[1] *Œuvres philosophiques*, Paris, 1927, I, 83.

> clings to Socialism, which utilizes science to dispel the smoke of religion, organizes the worker for his struggle to obtain better conditions on earth and frees him from belief in a life to come (p. 4).
>
> " 'Religion is the opium of the people.' These words of Marx form the corner-stone of the entire Marxist conception of religion. Modern churches and religions, religious organizations of all kinds, are always considered by Marxism to be organs of *bourgeois* reaction which serve to encourage exploitation and to brutify the working classes."

Marx and Engels were a little undecided about the most practical way of carrying on the war against religion, but it was always this objective that they kept in view. Engels thought that the organizing of the proletariat itself ought to lead to the annulment of religion. According to the definition of Marx, " the struggle against religion is indirectly the struggle against that world of which religion is the spiritual aroma." In 1869 he went farther. " The struggle against the priests must first and foremost be waged in Catholic countries."

But it was Lenin who converted this doctrine into an idea which was to influence the masses, created organizations and inspired them with a kind of mystical fervour directed against God.

> " No book of popular appeal will be able to expel religion from masses brutified by capitalist tyranny and subjected to the action of capitalism's blind destructive force until these masses have learned to organize themselves and to strive consciously, coherently and systematically to extirpate the very roots of religion and to destroy the domination of Capital, in every form " (p. 17).

As long previously as 1905 Lenin had enunciated the attitude of the Workers' Party to religion in these terms :

> " Every religious idea is an abomination. . . . We must combat religion ; that is the ABC of all materialism. . . . But Marxism says : One must *learn* to fight religion. . . . The strife against religion must not be confined to abstract

ideological preaching. . . . It must be bound up with the concrete practice of class movement, and lead to the destruction of the roots which religion has taken in society " (pp. 15–16).

After the victory of the Russian revolution of October 1917, Lenin had Marx's aphorism " Religion is the opium of the people " carved in enormous letters on a wall opposite the famous church of Our Lady of Iberia at Moscow. The idea has now become an obsession with the extremists, has eaten its way into the minds of revolutionary masses all over the world, and has transformed Marx's speculative and critical phrase into an idea of mysterious and explosive force, kindling the spirits of the proletariat in an anti-religious fury for destructive strife.

This is a form of mysticism which sunders souls from God, and finds expression in a sectarian organization for putting the most impious ideas into practice.

In due course Moscow created its International of the Godless, transforming atheism, for the first time in history, from a discursive kind of proselytizing force into an organized army, the aim of which is to destroy and expel from society every trace of religious reality and every divine idea that existed in individual souls. In every nation an atmosphere in which the war can be carried on is being prepared, and in every nation sufficient powder is being stored up so that, at the right moment, there may be an explosion of vandalism such as has occurred in no other revolution in the world's history.

" Among the objectives of the cultural revolution which most affect the masses," states the programme of the Communist International, " the strife against religion, that opium of the peoples, holds a special place ; this strife must be carried on inflexibly, implacably."

" Our atheism is a militant atheism," declared the Soviet organ, *Godless*, in August 1935. " There is no question of our living peaceably with clergy among us ; there must be an implacable war against religion for the re-education of the workers who still adhere to the Church. This is our aim : Increasing implacability against religion."

Such organizations and such slogans have not been ineffective. Not only has atheistic propaganda developed to an enormous extent, but " direct action " has struck continually, " inflexibly and implacably ", at what the Godless call the " social roots " of religion. The Soviet Union has revealed itself to the proletariat of the world as the chief instrument of destruction wielded by militant atheism.

One of the best informed and documented periodicals in Europe, the *Schoenere Zukunft*, of Vienna (April 17, 1937, No. 29), published an impressive summary of the principal work of the Godless in Russia.

Down to the middle of 1936, 42,800 Orthodox priests had been put out of action ; some of these were shot, others exiled to Siberia. In 1920, the Orthodox religious communities had some 2,000 monasteries and over 100,000 members ; these monasteries have all been confiscated and the number of the religious has been reduced to 30,000, most of whom are in prison or exile.

The hierarchy of the Catholic Church in the U.S.S.R. comprised eight Bishops and 810 parish priests—all long ago either expelled from the country or murdered. In 1936 alone, 800 Catholic priests were imprisoned ; 102 of these were executed and the remainder exiled.

As to Evangelical pastors, in 1917, Russia had 200 of these engaged in their ministry ; only four are now living.

Of late the persecution has been intensified. The Director of the Guepu has initiated a spectacular trial of the Metropolitan Theofanos and various other Orthodox Bishops who, with other members of the higher clergy, have recently been arrested. Altogether 112 priests are expecting to hear their death sentences. The Guepu has also arrested the last five Catholic priests who were still at liberty.

During 1937 many churches were closed for failing to produce the exorbitant sums of money demanded from the congregations, sums often quite beyond their means. The list of these churches includes 1,900 belonging to the Orthodox, 240 Catholic churches, 200 mosques, 115 synagogues, 61 Lutheran churches and various chapels belonging to other sects.

The fact that in many parts of Russia, after twenty years

of militant atheism, Christian worship has survived at all is explained, not only by the dimensions of the country, and the loneliness of the steppes, where State domination becomes almost impossible, but also, and principally, by the tenacity of the religious spirit in the Russian people. Instead of their "popes" they had now their "stariks," Christian pilgrims who escaped Soviet vigilance by taking up some secular occupation and went from one village to another preaching Christian doctrine. In many districts the local Soviets had to allow them to do this religious work openly so as not to exacerbate feeling among the peasants. Recently, however, persecution has been directed at these pilgrims also.

With no less frenzy does Soviet Russia wage war upon the observance of that greatest of all Russian festivals, Easter. Last year, in regions where the age-old Easter traditions have survived twenty years of persecution, over eight thousand anti-Christian lectures were arranged. During the days of Holy Week and Easter no bells are allowed to ring, and work goes on without a break all over the country. As a counter-attraction, large-scale military manœuvres, in which the Soviet youth-groups took part, were arranged for the same period. It has been estimated that some 200,000 of the Godless took an active part last year in the combat against the Christian Easter.

In Central Asia, the invasion of the Godless has assumed militant form against the mosques and the *mulahs* ; 10,000 Godless have been mobilized to break up Mohammedan festivals or otherwise to impede the cult of Islam.

The League of the Godless is incarnated in international Sovietic Bolshevism, on the model of which it bases its organization. In Leningrad alone there are 1,059 atheist "cells" with 24,326 militant members; in the outskirts of the same city, 241 cells, with 14,056 members. Recently the Secretary of the Central Committee of the Communist Party reported that a considerable number of members of the party did not belong to the Atheist League ; a decision was at once taken that any member who had not joined it within three months should be expelled from the Party.

It is this technical specialization which gives militant atheism in Soviet Russia its force and efficacy. Its cellular infiltration among the masses of the proletariat uproots all belief from individual souls, inspires them with hatred of God and facilitates popular mobilization against the Churches. The international character of atheistic organization universalizes the principles and methods of the Godless and at the same time assures the orthodoxy of Communistic materialism in all countries. Its outstanding position, as regards both doctrine and action, within the sphere of Sovietic Bolshevism gives it an importance comparable with that of the Komintern itself, whose inner councils are invariably coloured by militant atheism. Thus atheism and revolutionary politics have achieved a kind of mutual interpenetration.

Russia, declares the Political Commissariat of the Interior, must become the first country in the world to have no priests. " War against Fascism ", wrote *Godless*, the official organ of the Atheist League, three months before the Spanish Revolution, " is at the same time war against religion and priestcraft."

The slogan soon became familiar in Spain, where the Godless lost no time in putting it into practice. Lenin had prophesied that Spain was to become the second country in Europe to be bolshevized. Could it not also become the second country in the world to have no priests ?

Anyone who makes an objective search for the origins of the religious persecution in Spain will at once find them here, and need waste no time in discussing isolated incidents and anecdotes both tragic and picturesque. A closer examination will reveal the twin sources of the Revolution —Marxism in its different branches and Anarchism in its two great organisms known as the National Confederation of Labour (C.N.T.) and the Iberian Anarchist Federation (F.A.I.), both of which have their beginnings in atheistic and materialistic ideology.

The Marxist current is heavily charged with Muscovite mysticism. Bukharin's widely diffused *ABC of Communism* supplied the masses with a central thesis : " Both in theory and in practice religion and Communism are incompatible."

When we come to facts, this slogan finds expression in incendiarism and extermination.

Anarchism, the outbreak of which in a Bakuninist form during the Spanish Revolution of 1873–4 left the south of Spain and the east coast as far as Valencia infected with nihilistic doctrine, has had an indescribably potent influence on the proletarian masses and the doctrines of its leaders—Bakunin, Kropotkin, Reclus and Malatesta—have enjoyed the widest diffusion. By the intermediacy of an efficient and aggressive form of Syndicalism the machinery of Anarchism was set up in Spain, principally in Catalonia and Aragon.

The age-long anti-religious fury of the authors of Anarchism had nothing to learn from the Muscovite development of Marxist atheism. The so-called " Libertarians " of to-day know by heart all that is implied in Bakunin's rancorous dictum: " Church and State are the two black beasts: we must crush them ! " They all bear, written upon their hearts, the brief summary of their creed, dynamic rather than doctrinal: " In practice as in theory the Anarchist is the enemy of religion, capitalism and the State. He thus wages three simultaneous wars against Authority. His blows spare neither the State nor Property nor Religion. He suppresses all three."

> " We desire not only to abolish all forms of authority but to destroy them simultaneously, every one. We proclaim this total and simultaneous destruction to be inevitable."[1]

The definition is certainly clear enough, and Sebastien Faure, its author, must have been gratified when he visited Barcelona and found it in a state of what the revolutionaries call " complete Anarchist order," to see how faithfully his Spanish disciples had interpreted his teachings.

When the origins of the Proletarian Revolution are so alive with tragic reality and so clearly set forth for any critic and observer to read, how can anyone, Spaniard or foreigner, close his eyes to the light, and, while calling himself a Catholic, even conceive ascribing the responsibilities and

[1] *Encyclopédie anarchiste*, I, 84 (" Anarchie ", by Sebastien Faure).

horrors of the Revolution to a handful of alleged facts, at most isolated and of doubtful veracity, the influence of which, in this case, has quite clearly been small, if indeed there has been any at all ?

This, then, is our first reply to the accusation formulated above.

Let us bear in mind how for years the ideas already described had been diffused by proletarian organizations, how they obtained currency in the extremist publications of the revolutionary parties, how the anti-religious campaigns of these parties made play with anti-clerical pretences and inculcated hatred of God. If we could enumerate all the acts of vandalism committed during the five years of Republican demagogy we should have a fairly exact idea of the progressive poisoning of the minds of the masses, which went on for so long that the extremists had nothing more to do than to await their opportunity.

As the moment drew near, further stimuli were applied to the minds of the proletariat.

It is now common knowledge that the Atheist League had arranged in its preliminary programme of the Revolution for a plebiscite to be held as to what was to be done with churches and presbyteries throughout Spain. Less generally known is the fact that, a few weeks before the outbreak of the Revolution, the C.N.T. held its National Congress at Saragossa and that among its resolutions was one proclaiming the uselessness of churches and advocating the prohibition of public worship on the grounds that anyone desirous of troubling himself about God could do so in the intimacy of his conscience or in the temple of Nature.

On July 17, 1936, the day before the Revolution began, a Valencian periodical called *La Traca* published replies, submitted by its readers, to the question : " What would you do with the cassocked gentry (*la gente de sotana*) ? " Two pages of this issue, reproduced in the German " Red Book on Spain ",[1] contain 346 of the answers received from towns and villages all over the country. They are unbelievably crude, barbarous and sadistic, often even homicidal. Let

[1] *Das Rotbuch über Spanien* (Berlin, Leipzig, 1937), p. 90, which gives the pages in facsimile.

one of the most elegant of them serve as a typical example: "I would hang the monks with the entrails of the priests." In the event, even verbal bestialities of the type of this proved translatable into reality.

Some may say that these explosions of homicidal hatred were mere outlets for the feelings: even were this true they would not be without their significance. But unhappily almost every one of these inhuman desires that it was possible to translate into practice has been so translated. Beneath the full sunlight of the Revolution germs of every crime rapidly ripen and grow. "Revolution, that solstice of crime!" as Lamartine put it.

Nor must it be forgotten that, during the revolution of October 6, 1934, "black lists" of sinister and significant import were discovered even in the smallest villages. Many more were found two years later. The drawing-up of them was the last of the preparations for an epoch of religious persecution unique in the history of Christianity.

CHAPTER III

THE CHURCHES WHICH WERE USED AS FORTRESSES AND THE CLERGY WHO FIRED ON THE PEOPLE

COMING now to the main accusation launched by the Church's enemies, we find that the chief difficulty in answering it is the lack of evidence by which it is accompanied. Hardly any is adduced by the " nine-Catholic " group, which represents, as it were, the right wing of the accusers ; nor is there any more from the group of French Communist intellectuals, its very vocal left wing, which has concentrated its attention chiefly upon Barcelona.

For an accusation of such gravity this lack of evidence is surprising. Señor Semprún, for example, quotes the testimony of an unnamed " young friend " of his who, on July 21, 1936, saw three priests under arms at a Navarran village called Lesaca. Another is said to have been imprisoned and shot by the Reds. A certain " Don Mónico " is alleged to have been leading a column in the province of Guipúzcoa. Even supposing these charges to have been true, however, they could not possibly, in the nature of the case, have provoked the religious persecution.

But it was from Barcelona that foreign propagandists imported most of their detailed descriptions of churches which had been used as fortresses and of clergy firing upon the people. On August 29, 1936, there appeared a most impressive special number of the French periodical *Vu*, the object of which was to draw up an extensive apologia for the Proletarian Revolution.[1] One of the questions asked of a number of witnesses and answered by them at length in this issue was : " Why have the churches been burned ? " Here are some of the replies.

The first witness, G. Soria, describes the great battle of

[1] *Vu en Espagne : la défense de la République.*

July 19 in the Barcelona streets, which he claims to have seen with his own eyes, as follows:

> "In all parts of that agitated city, on that morning of July 19, men dressed in cassocks or habits hurried to exchange their rosaries for machine-guns, to convert their churches or chapels into nests bristling with rifles and munitions. . . . The principal quarter in which the rebels occupied churches and convents, which they turned into fortresses, was that maze of narrow streets lying to the left of the Ramblas and between them and the Harbour. . . . The Fascists barricaded themselves in the Church of Santa María del Mar, whence, seconded by their priests, they fired upon the people. . . . Let me say once more that *all the churches which have been burned had contained Fascists*."[1]

This, were it not so tragic, would be laughable. Apart from the incorrect topographical description of the Barcelona fighting on that day, what can one say of the extraordinary picture of the legion of armed men in habits, "in all parts of that agitated city," whom nobody else appears to have seen but this one foreigner!

The evidence given by two other witnesses, J. R. Bloch and Jean Cassou, is too vague for refutation. Another, J. E. Pouterman, describes a group of militiamen three of whom he alleges to have been wounded in a surprise attack from a church—"a magnificent specimen of Spanish Baroque art"—which they had been ordered to leave unharmed. The man in charge of the group, according to his story, sent to ask for instructions and left the church untouched until he received definite orders to reduce it. The name of the church treated with such magnanimity is not given; but the obvious one to fit the description, as anyone acquainted with Barcelona knows, is Belén, and here no such thing could possibly have happened.

Further, a certain Minister of the Catalan Government is quoted as attributing the outbreak of popular fury to the fact that the people had been fired upon "from two churches".

[1] Op. cit., p. 48.

What a procedure! From the alleged happenings in "two churches" (unnamed) in Barcelona we are invited to deduce the generalization that the whole of the Spanish clergy, if not the Church as a whole, was responsible for, or consenting to, the revolt of the Army! Such reasoning alone should suffice to invalidate the entire campaign.

Continuing, however, our search for facts, we eventually discover a large and resounding one, the existence of which cannot be gainsaid—the case of the Carmelite Fathers of the Gran Vía Diagonal, whose monastery, without the slightest doubt, figured in the fighting. How can this be accounted for?

What happened was that, on the eve of the battle (for which both sides had made preparations), the superiors of the monastery refused decisively, not only to harbour soldiers but even to defend the building itself, though it was likely to be in the direct line of attack. When the fighting began, soldiers driven back by Government forces upon the monastery invaded it and remained in it until on the next day they saw that they had lost the battle. That it was never used, in the strict sense, for military purposes can be proved by the testimony of many people who attended services in the chapel as late as the evening of July 18, and by that of several of the friars who succeeded in escaping from the country.

The Prior, who was among these, has related the whole story in such detail as to leave no room for error. The Colonel of the insurgent battalion came to him in person to ask him if he would give shelter to his wounded. The Prior hesitated; the Colonel became more insistent; in the end the Prior gave in. At a later stage of the battle he had no say in the matter, for, when the fighting began to go against them, the Colonel returned with one hundred and fifty soldiers—this time to stay. At eleven o'clock on the next day an officer of the Civil Guard entered the monastery to demand the Colonel's surrender. Before he obtained it, however, guarantees were given for the lives of the insurgent soldiers and of the friars.[1]

So much for the case of the Diagonal. We know of no

[1] *L'Aurora del SS. Sacramento*, Milan, Gennaio, 1937.

other of which so much capital has been made anywhere in Spain. In Madrid the only notable case was that of the Basilica of Atocha, from the tower of which, as also from the roofs of a number of houses, soldiers defended the old María Cristina barracks on the Monday morning of the Madrid rebellion.[1] When the barracks had been surrendered, a horde of enraged militiamen poured into the Dominican Monastery, accusing the Fathers of having fired at them from the church tower. Fortunately they were met by one of the Fathers, a man of resolute character and great presence of mind, who was able to prove to them irrefutably that all the monks were in the house and that they had not a single weapon among them. The militiamen, duly convinced, went quietly away, though some of the Fathers were subsequently murdered in the streets by the mobs.

No doubt there are parallel cases of less importance. But even if it can be proved that churches here and there were occupied by soldiers or civilians, it in no way follows that this was done with the consent of the secular or the regular clergy concerned. In Barcelona, for example, the fiercest part of the battle centred around the Hotel Colón, the Telephone Building and the University; both these buildings and many private houses were commandeered by the one side or the other. Yet from these facts nobody generalizes as to the complicity of the occupants or owners. Later in the War, in Vizcaya and other regions, strategical exigences again and again made it necessary to ignore the sanctity of religious edifices. In every kind of war the same thing occurs. The fact is deplorable, but what can possibly be deduced from it? Only this: that the Church, now as always, is the victim of human violence and passion.

It will perhaps be of interest if we now look at the other side of the picture and set down some of the facts which clearly disprove the truth of these accusations.

In Barcelona, on the morning of Sunday, July 19, 1936, there was little general realization of the gravity of the events that were taking place, as was perhaps natural in a city of over a million inhabitants. It is not surprising,

[1] [This took place on Monday, July 20, 1936, and resulted in the defeat of the Army and the surrender and execution of its leaders.—Tr.]

therefore, that in many of the churches the Sunday morning services should have been held as usual, and even that, as late as eleven o'clock, Mass should have been celebrated in a few of those centrally situated.

It was about midday that the revolutionaries began to show themselves in their true colours by setting fire to a number of the more important churches, situated in parts of the city in which there had been no fighting—notably the parish churches of Bonanova, San Pedro de las Puellas, Santa María del Mar, San Miguel del Puerto, all of which were situated in a line well out of the area of the fighting. This incendiarism was the work of separate groups of revolutionaries, and it is a striking fact that the attacks were made almost simultaneously. During the evening more fires were started, and they can hardly be said to have ceased until the whole of the Catalan churches were devastated, even to the tiny sanctuaries which crown the hill-tops in that country.

In the beautiful mediæval church of Santa María del Mar the priest who habitually celebrated the five o'clock Mass on Sunday mornings did so as usual. It so happened, however, that he was unwell, so, after the service, he went back to his house, which was near at hand. A few hours later a group of armed men came to take him away, saying that he had been firing on the people from the church tower. Fortunately he found plenty of witnesses who could absolve him, and, yielding to the force of their testimony, the men left him in peace. But this did not save Santa María del Mar from partial destruction.

In the parish church of Bonanova, some miles from the centre of the city, the ten o'clock Mass was said as usual, but it was noticed that a few suspiciously undevout men were present. These men, as it afterwards transpired, were awaiting the arrival of an automobile carrying incendiary bombs, with which they were proposing to set fire to the church. The automobile, however, had met with an accident: in the Avenue of the Argentine Republic, to be precise, it had collided with a standard, the bombs had exploded, and only the driver remained alive to tell the tale. The burning of the church had, therefore, to be postponed until noon. At this hour the square in front of the church was occupied by armed men who had arrived on lorries bearing the initials F.A.I. and C.N.T. Entering the presbytery, they seized seven priests who had taken refuge there. As these were all well known in that particular suburb, they were given up, through the intervention of the people themselves, to the police, who saved their lives by passing them over to the Director-General of Public Order.

In San Pedro de las Puellas, the church door was closed for greater safety while Mass was being said, but the explosion of a bomb interrupted the service and the celebrant had hurriedly to leave, by the door communicating with the church, for the adjacent presbytery. Here he deposited the sacred ornaments and escaped. He did well, for that evening, when the church of Santa Monica was set on fire, a priest who happened to be there was murdered.

At nine o'clock that night a crowd attempted to force an entry into the church of Belén, whereupon the priest, who was acting as sacristan, in the hope of avoiding damage, opened the door for them. Their first act was to shoot him, after which they set to work systematically to destroy that " magnificent specimen of Spanish Baroque art ", the beauty of which has been sufficiently expatiated upon, in a passage quoted above, by defenders of the revolutionaries who destroyed it.

From the nightfall of that Sunday onwards, while fighting was still proceeding in the streets, there began the great round-up of priests and devout laymen of all classes. " Spaniards of right-wing opinions ", as *Solidaridad Obrera* said over a year later,[1] were considered to be " incompatible with any kind of democratic legality, and indeed *impossible for human beings to live with, because they are Catholics.*"

Carrying lists of their intended victims, with the fullest details concerning whom they were often provided, these highly organized groups set off gleefully on their man-hunts. Throughout that night those Bonanova priests who had been arrested in their cassocks at the end of a service and carried off to prison, heard again and again the wild cry of " Another

[1] August 27, 1937. [*Solidaridad Obrera* is one of the most notorious of the Syndicalist organs in Spain.—Tr.]

priest!" All over the city revolutionary centres were quickly converted into clandestine prisons. But many of those who were being taken to them—failed to arrive.

The way in which the persecution was begun on that very Sunday when the prime necessity was to overcome the military revolt was itself an irrefutable revelation of the origins of the Revolution. We have learned of a number of cases which prove with what care the lists of the intended victims had been compiled: addresses, professions, particulars of entire families—everything was complete. The searches were carried out by committees, and each was responsible for rounding up all priests whose work lay within the area assigned to it. Some of these priests, holding well-known official positions, have told us that they were searched for by different committees in three or four places.

Often arms were hidden by the searchers in the houses they were examining so that they could return after a brief interval and discover so-called proofs of guilt.

Another common ruse was to fire a round under the pretext of self-defence against aggression. On the first Tuesday of the Revolution this was done in Barcelona during the burning of the convent of Nuestra Señora de la Enseñanza.

In the parish of San Boy de Llobregat some militiamen went to find the priest and ordered him to open the church for them. As they were going along, the wary and rather fearful priest remarked:

"Now, fair play! And don't fire and then say that you were fired on from the church, as has been done elsewhere."

The following incident took place in a large town on the Mediterranean coast. Near the Court House was a parish which contained a great many revolutionaries. The church was fired upon on the Sunday night (July 19), and attempts were made to burn it. The three priests who lived together in the presbytery took refuge in a house near by. On the Monday evening the house was suddenly invaded by a gang of men who declared their intention of burning the church down "because we have just seen the rector and his assistant priests firing from it." The rector and his assistant priests, who had been in this very house since the previous night, had just time to hear this surprising news before once more making their escape and thus avoiding what would have been the inevitable consequences of their "attack" on the "people".

There were actually persons shameless enough to declare that a cassocked priest had been discovered firing from the tower—some said of Barcelona Cathedral, some of Santa María del Mar—and that those who discovered him had cut off his head. What a trophy it would have been had the thing ever happened! But, of course, it had not happened. The rumour, however, was so widespread that a group of people went up to the Cathedral towers to look round, the Cathedral itself having been closed from the first day of the Revolution. The Catalan Government also sent a squad of soldiers to inspect the towers. Neither of the parties knew that the other was there: it was fortunate, when they suddenly came upon each other on the roof of the cloisters, that neither fired! No one, needless to say, found the decapitated body of a priest—but the legend went on merrily, none the less.

It must be remembered that this game of pretexts is an old trick of traditional anti-clericalism. In France, throughout the year 1937, there were cases of agitations against churches and religious houses, the reasons given for these being that stores of arms had been found or Fascist meetings held in them. The Bishops concerned made public declarations to the contrary and the falsity of the charges was soon proved. The legend, however, was started on its way, and will no doubt be frequently heard again in the future.

There is another famous example of the same thing in recent Spanish history concerning the beginnings of that era of religious persecution under the Second Republic which reached its climax when the Popular Front came into power.

At the time of the church-burnings of May 1931 in southern and eastern Spain, the Government freed itself, as it considered, from all responsibility for them, by attributing these excesses to the fact that the Monarchists had held a meeting in Madrid, which, they said, had provoked them. Now in President Azaña's *Secret and Private Memoirs*, a manuscript volume which found its way into hands very different from those for which it was intended, and has been published in facsimile by the Nationalists, there is a most illuminating entry dated December 7, 1932 :

> " ' Casares[1] came too. The Police department has just learned, in confidence, that there will be riots at the University to-morrow, and that, while they are going on, mobs will try to set some religious houses on fire. The person from whom the information comes is the same who gave Maura[2] advance information about the incendiarism in May of last year.'
>
> " ' Oh, didn't you know that Maura was informed about that forty-eight hours beforehand and took no notice of the warning ? '
>
> " ' No, I certainly did not.' "

[1] [Señor Casares Quiroga, afterwards Prime Minister in the Popular Front Government of 1936.—Tr.]

[2] [Don Miguel Maura, Republican Home Secretary at the time of the riots of May 1931.—Tr.]

CHAPTER IV

THE ORGANIZATION OF ANARCHY AND THE TECHNIQUE OF PERSECUTION

WAS all this violence attributable to the righteous anger of the "people"? Was it blind vengeance, because the churches had been used for firing on the "people"? There is not a fact that can be cited in support of these assertions, not a name that can be brought forward in evidence, not a shred of proof.

On that Sunday, July 19, 1936, the "people", in the ordinary sense of the word, were not out of doors at all. Those who were in the streets consisted of definitely organized groups who were carrying out their acts of vandalism in the very presence of those usually known as the "forces of law and order". There had been the most detailed preparation for it all; there was an executive to organize it; and there were orders methodically carried out. Had it all been genuinely the work of the people, even of a people misled and excited by the absurd legends that were current, this would soon have become clear from the very nature of the excesses themselves: there would have been more exceptional cases where no harm was done, through the good sense of the crowds and the respect or pity felt by them for their victims. In numbers of towns, the people, in the true sense, did defend, or attempt to defend, their parish priests: had they, and not revolutionary committees, with their Terror-technique, been at the bottom of the persecution, the consequences of such acts would not have been so unfortunate, and often so tragic.

Above all, the devastation, and the ferocity of it, would not have been so rapid and so nearly uniform throughout the country. The *people*, in the true sense, could not have "standardized" a persecution, not only all over Catalonia, but all over Spain, bearing the same essential marks of savagery and the lust foı extermination ; even in Vizcaya, where there were good reasons why it should be restrained, we find a repetition of the same horrible acts.

Those who have witnessed the deeds of vandalism committed in Catalonia need no further proofs of this. Many thousands of horror-struck citizens have watched the *caravanas técnicas* of incendiarism and crime at work at Vich, Igualada, Sabadell, Tarrasa, Montserrat, Manresa, Solsona, Seo de Urgel, Gerona, Lérida, Tarragona, and even in the high Pyrenean valleys and the Valle de Arán, far from the principal scenes of revolutionary uproar.

At Vich, a cathedral city in Catalonia and an important centre of religious life, there arrived, on the morning of Tuesday, July 21, a number of lorries full of men quite unknown in the district. In the great central square of the city they drew up, and the leader of the band, mounting a lorry, cried: "In two hours' time Vich will be burning from end to end." Then the men got busy with great rapidity. Well provided with bombs and petrol, they set to work on the churches and religious houses ; profaned the tombs of saints and other great figures of the Church, such as Balmes and Toıras y Bages, going so far as to play football with the latter's head. They destroyed the marvellous paintings of José María Sert and set fire to the magnificent Diocesan Museum ; only the courage of a few determined individuals prevented the latter from being completely destroyed. In the same way other individuals saved the thousand-year-old Basilica of Ripoll, which was also attacked by the mobs.

That these church-burners were men specially detailed for their tasks might be proved by describing a very large number of incidents, of which one must suffice. After the capture of Bilbao by the Nationalists in June 1937, there was found in the Commissariat of Police a document which had belonged to a certain Eduardo Suárez. It read as follows:

> "The bearer of this safe-conduct is to be given no other work to do, as he is employed on the destruction of churches."

This safe-conduct had been issued at Gijón in October 1936, and bore the seals of the Syndicalist (C.N.T.) and Anarchist (F.A.I.) unions and those of other Libertarian groups in that city.

A number of armed cars coming from La Torrasa (Hospitalet), a place which had been invaded by a rabble of immigrants from other parts of Spain, engaged in a hunt for the Cardinal Archbishop of Tarragona. It was not till the Wednesday of that first week of the persecution (July 22) that they found him in the Monastery of Poblet. They were under orders to shoot him by the wayside; but the Christian serenity and meekness with which he met them completely disarmed them—in the literal sense of the word—and they let him go.

The terrible slaughter which took place at Lérida is notorious: the gentle Bishop, Dr. Huix, died at the head of a group of clergy and laity, quietly giving his blessing to all before they shot him. In the same city, on the evening of Monday, July 20, the parish priest of the church of San Lorenzo, dressed in lay clothes, was looking for a hiding-place when some women and boys recognized him and cried, "Kill him! Kill him!" He turned to flee but three militiamen coming from the opposite direction shot him on the spot, amid the shouts of a crowd which had assembled.

On the Tuesday (July 21), in Seo de Urgel, the most peaceful cathedral city in Catalonia, the news went round that bands of incendiaries from another town were approaching. The Bishop, an old man popular even with left-wing extremists, was actually persuaded by these extremists to leave his palace in haste, and, after being searched, was taken in lay attire to the Andorran frontier.[1]

The Auxiliary Bishop of Tarragona was seized and taken to Montblanc Prison. Neither the goodwill nor the strenuous efforts of those in authority sufficed to save him. He was shot on the Coll de Lilla, and his dead body was burned.

It was thus that the "people" treated leaders of the Church for whom the people, in the true sense, had nothing but respect and affection.

[1] [Seo de Urgel is only a few miles from the small republic of Andorra, which was, of course, neutral ground.—Tr.]

Are any further proofs needed that the persecution was an organized movement ?

Then let us describe what happened in Barcelona after Anarchists, Syndicalists and Communists had usurped the organization of the new "revolutionary order" under the very eyes of the autonomous Government of Catalonia, which had lost effective control over the people, and was as much the victim of the Terror as any ordinary citizen.

On the Monday of the Revolution (July 20) these extremist groups were incessantly broadcasting orders by radio. The theme of one of the most ardent of their exhortations was that Fascism and the Church were one and the same thing and that the latter must be exterminated before the former could be defeated. Indeed, they went farther than this. "The Church must be destroyed," they cried, "and everything that has any connection with it. What does it matter if the churches are artistic monuments ? The good militiaman will not hesitate for a moment. The Church must be destroyed ! "

El Socialista, a Madrid newspaper, published a similar incitement to destruction. "Do not hesitate, militiamen, to destroy these buildings, whatever their value as works of art, for each of them is one thing more taken from the enemy."[1]

Occasionally, as for example at the time of the collective assassinations at Tarrasa, the revolutionaries themselves seemed to be panic-stricken when they viewed their handiwork ; but on other occasions each outrage stimulated them to further efforts. An aeroplane flying over the town at this time dropped leaflets which read : "The Revolution is going to drown us all in blood." Attempts were made to prevent any slackening of violence and incitements to crime, such as the following, taken from the Revolution's official organ, *Solidaridad Obrera*, were frequent :

> "We have rounded up all the priests and parasites ; we have driven away all who have not already died with arms in their hands—and they will never return. We have dealt faithfully with the follies of the Church and its so-called charity, and with the clergy who, while

[1] Cit. *Gringoire*, January 22, 1937.

giving themselves out to be apostles of peace, had been sacrificing the sons of the people to the great monopolizers of riches and the purloiners of freedom.

" We have kindled our torches and applied the purifying fire to all the churches—those monuments which for years had been casting their shadows over every corner of Spain —and we have traversed the entire country-side, and purified it from the plague of religion."

On October 18, 1936, *Solidaridad Obrera* published another article entitled " Blood and Fire " :

" Continually, at all times and in all places, the most horrible crimes have been committed with the Cross as a mute witness. . . . Not a single church has been left standing in Barcelona, and it may be assumed that they will not be restored and that pickaxe and hammer will complete the demolition of what the fire began by purifying. But what about the villages ? Not only must not a single one of the cassocked blackbeetles be left but we must eradicate any germs which they may have incubated. Destruction, then ! Not a moment's hesitation ! Blood and fire ! "

Then there were the famous trick-photographs of clergy bearing arms, and other revolutionary propaganda.

In the first days of the Revolution a number of religious and priests were run to ground at Igualada, given arms, placed in position near a monastery and forced to point their rifles as though they were firing. Some of them saw the hidden cameras photographing them while they did so.

One day, a person who has since been able to escape from Spain was walking along one of the narrow, mediæval streets of Gerona and, to his unspeakable surprise, saw a little procession of clergy bearing arms and striking warlike attitudes, exactly as though they were going off to fight. As they approached, a cinematograph operator came into view working his camera !

On another occasion a number of priests and religious who were in a Barcelona prison found themselves, to their great astonishment, served with rifles. Revolver in hand, a group of militiamen made them climb a staircase and then come down again with their rifles raised as though they were preparing to fire. As they did so the cinematograph operator "surprised" these dastardly revolutionaries: his films were no doubt most useful for propaganda.

These and similar facts have been gleaned direct from witnesses—some of whom saw the film-comedies while others took part in them against their will. No doubt they did a great deal to propagate the legend of the clergy who fired on the "people" and the churches turned into fortresses. In Barcelona alone over two hundred and twenty churches or large chapels were pillaged and burned. Imagine what a splendid ecclesiastical war museum could have been founded —if any arms had indeed been found in them! We may well wonder why the French Communists who, in the pages of *Vu*, described militiamen and workers hastening to present the authorities with valuable articles used in worship as a proof of their friendliness to religion, did not also see with their own eyes the finding of all this war material in the churches or the clergy caught in the act of firing on the people!

Yet these calumnies are repeated even by those in authority. Luis Companys, President of the Catalan Government, must be very well aware of what happened in Barcelona. Yet when, at the end of August, 1936, a correspondent of *L'Œuvre*, in an interview with him, mentioned the religious problem—not without some hesitation, in view of the delicacy of the subject—Señor Companys justified the excesses committed in the preceding month by the alleged participation of the clergy in the rebellion. On being asked what possibility there was of reopening the Catholic churches for worship, he replied: "Oh, that problem doesn't even exist: all the churches have been destroyed!"

Although in this chapter we have spoken chiefly of Catalonia, similar events took place in other parts of Spain: in Madrid, for example, nineteen churches were profaned during the first two days of the Revolution. But Catalonia provides the best example of the nature of this persecution of religion. Only in Barcelona was there any military rising, and there it was put down in twenty-four hours. In the rest of Catalonia not a shot was fired: at Lérida the garrison surrendered almost without resistance. Further, there was no pressing "religious question" in Catalonia; apart from some anti-clerical violence in the elections of January, 1934, and a few isolated cases in the rebellion of the following October, there were no attacks made upon religion, as there were in other parts of Spain, either in the five months of Popular Front government or in the entire history of the Second Republic.

Yet, notwithstanding this, the destruction of the churches was as complete here as elsewhere, the revolutionary *régime* as triumphant, the religious persecution as ferocious, the social collapse as grave and the collectivist experiment as baneful.

From the shipwreck of a Catalonia denaturalized and oppressed by the anti-patriotic and demagogic Esquerra[1] only two things can be salvaged—two noble traits to which we gladly render homage. One of them is the heroic devotion of a group of officials who, not without peril to themselves, rescued a considerable part of the archæological and religious patrimony of our country. The other is the generous and effective goodwill with which certain persons in authority contrived to save the lives of those who found themselves in grave danger yet whose ideas they did not share. This latter service deserves the greater praise because the rescuers, as a result of their action, became themselves obliged to leave the country in order to save their lives.

Perhaps, however, in strict justice, it may be said that something more has been saved. The real Catalonia is still in existence—a Catalonia temperamentally and ideally anti-revolutionary, neither separatist nor libertarian, loving culture, tradition, order, authority and justice. This Catalonia has been contaminated neither by the spirit of the Revolution nor by its works, and it has neither perished nor become engulfed in chaos by Republican demagogism nor Anarcho-Muscovite tyranny, which, both before and after July 19, 1936, attempted to destroy the State and to annihilate Spanish society body and soul. Christian Catalonia is still in being; her latent energy and vigour are stronger

[1] [The Esquerra is the left-wing Catalan Nationalist Party, whose leader is Señor Companys.—Tr.]

than ever before, and throughout the terrible persecution which she has suffered she has continued to tread the paths of saintliness—a saintliness silent in affliction, active in charity and heroic in death.

Such has been the history of Catalonia. Torn and bleeding as she is from the wounds inflicted by the War and the Revolution, she has been libelled abroad by fictions proceeding from the governments of Madrid, Barcelona and Bilbao and trodden under foot at home by the Red rabble. But, as will yet be seen, she survives with all her spiritual realism and generous loyalty, and she has many gifts to bring to the New Spain which has already triumphed over the Revolution.

CHAPTER V

PSYCHOLOGY OF THE ANARCHO-COMMUNIST REVOLUTION

It must not be thought that it is a waste of time to make a minute examination into the facts of the Revolution, since those who have laid such grave charges at our door are so anxious to leave facts aside and to spread absurd stories, completely devoid of foundation, about bishops leading columns of rebel soldiers to battle. If we were dealing with reasonable people who honestly desired to arrive at the truth it would be another matter, but unfortunately there is as much perversity as intrepidity in the charges being brought against the Church in Spain. If our calumniators were simply the Church's habitual enemies, one could understand their attempting to justify their awful massacres by such obvious falsehoods as the assertion, made by Cassou and others, that " priests were indeed killed during the fighting, but almost exclusively those who had taken an active part in it, either by themselves bearing arms or by lending their aid to the rebels in some other way." But unfortunately the perversity comes from other quarters, and is more abominable than this.

An attempt was made to reply to the *Joint Letter* of the Spanish bishops by a so-called " Group of Spanish priests." This was a new addition to the pseudo-Catholic forces, and it has done much abroad to disturb the right understanding and natural sympathy with the Church which would normally be felt by large sections of international opinion. With a tenacity and a zeal worthy of a better cause, they have circulated their " reply " all over France—even in the smallest parishes. One could wish that the authors were not the priests they claim to be ; unhappily, it seems impossible to explain the " reply " with such ease.[1]

[1] *La Carta Colectiva de los Obispos españoles.* The French version is published by *L.A.E.* (7 Boulevard Haussmann, Paris.) As preface it has

The original campaign of the intellectuals so closely connected with French Communism produced no impression, after its initial outburst, except in pro-Communist circles. The agitation of the " group of the nine Catholics " in favour of the so-called " Government " of Spain found all the doors that mattered closed to it everywhere.

In England the " Group of Anglican and Free Churchmen " who spent a few days in Spain and saw nothing much wrong with regard to religion but found proofs of tolerance on every side have been discounted by their own leaders and by all Christian opinion. Their visit was somewhat like the visit to Rome said to have been made by six Christians in the early years of Church history. They accepted the hospitality of Nero and afterwards reported to Jerusalem that, although he had forced the Christians to take refuge in the catacombs, he would be very happy to grant them full freedom when the situation was again normal. But it is with real grief that one has seen Catholic priests repeating the worst calumnies which sectarianism has brought against the Church and her ministers.

Let us pass over the lack of compassion which they have shown to their brethren who have been victims of the persecution and merely expose their arguments, the falsity of which we have already demonstrated :

> " During the first days of the Revolution both priests and churches were treated with absolute respect.
>
> " Firing against the people took place from various churches and monasteries in different cities.
>
> " Weapons and barricades were found in churches and monasteries.
>
> " It is as clear as daylight that before the military rebellion took place the lives of all priests were entirely respected, and that, if any were killed after the rebellion had taken place, it was due to the fact that, rightly or wrongly, the people believed them to be the allies and accomplices of the military rebels.

an article from *Euzko Deya*, the Basque paper, published in Paris, which has taken a leading part in the campaign of the clergy and self-styled Catholic laity against the Church in Spain.

"The persons of nuns were respected, almost without exception, even after the incendiarism and the slaughter had begun."

We might note particularly the unfortunate reference to the nuns, by which these supporters of the Revolution endeavour to excuse themselves. It is certain that several hundred nuns were killed. In any case, the pamphleteers would have done much better to keep silence about them, for the revolutionaries committed sadistic outrages of all kinds upon the persons of women, and did anything but respect those dedicated to the religious life. As to their other assertions, the vagueness of which will not pass unobserved, one might accept, for the sake of argument, the possibility that, in a few individual cases, such things may have occurred. But even then one would have to examine the circumstances, which they have not done, and, furthermore, one would have to prove that there was religious or ecclesiastical initiative or participation in the matter. The best proof of their mythical nature is the complete failure of the Red press to give any details about them, either in Madrid or in Barcelona. Even in publications where every effort has been made to bring together evidence which will discredit the religious character of National Spain, where the most diligent search for material has been carried out and truth has been strained to the utmost, only two of the so-called "fortress-churches" are named: the Seminary at Belchite and the church of Villarreal.[1] Again, it is curious that if the clergy fired on the people from the churches, not a single trial of such a cleric has been reported among the thousands of trials described in the Republican press. They might at least have arranged a mock trial or two of the kind, with cinematograph operators in attendance.

What can one say of the outrageous assertion that "before the military rebellion took place the lives of all priests were entirely respected"? Surely even abroad it is common knowledge that numerous and shameful outrages were perpetrated on the persons of priests, monks and nuns,

[1] [Both these refer to a date much later than that of the outbreak of the Revolution.—Tr.]

almost from the day of the accession of the Popular Front to power, especially in the eastern districts of Spain, in various parts of Andalusia and in Galicia. In the latter region alone, between the elections of February 16, 1936, and the outbreak of war on July 18, two priests were assassinated, fifty-eight were subjected to insults or physical violence, several were beaten, others were expelled from their parishes and others were threatened with death. In Madrid all kinds of outrages took place as the result of the fable that nuns had been giving children poisoned caramels. Or what about the forty priests, religious, seminarists and novices tortured and martyred during the Asturian rebellion of October 1934 (to say nothing of a few similar cases in the Catalonian rebellion of that month), which was a kind of rehearsal for the persecution of 1936? In the Asturian persecutions one saw all the marks of the beast. Some were mutilated, others slowly roasted to death, others soaked with benzine and set on fire—and so on. In one of the towns of Asturias the body of a priest was quartered, hung in a butcher's shop and labelled *Carne de cerno* ("pig's flesh"). But at that time nobody had thought of saying that priests had fired on the Asturian miners from the churches, the 1934 rebellion against the State having been begun and carried out by the Socialists for reasons that were purely political.

Rather than allow themselves to utter such falsehoods, it would be more to the point if the detractors of the Church declared that they are basing their actions on Rousseau's principles of the absolute goodness of the people and that they believe that the revolutionaries are in a state of grace!

But if one starts from the principle of the *sanctity* of the Revolution and of its hatred of religion; if one proposes to make a point of forgetting that the bestial element in man always comes to the surface in every revolution; if one closes one's eyes voluntarily to the visible and operative causes of that aggressive hatred of God which is to be found in the beginning and the development of the Spanish persecution—in that case it would be better to cease discussing hypothetical facts and to proclaim one's adherence, pure and simple, to the legitimacy of the nihilistic principles of the Revolution.

For in a catastrophic phenomenon of such a widespread and monstrous character, no quantity of anecdotes, however numerous, well-founded and logically convincing they may be, will suffice to provide the necessary relation between cause and effect. The characteristics of a revolution always proceed from deep-lying causes of a general character rooted in a collective state of mind and in a systematic orientation of tendencies skilfully directed by the leaders toward the destruction of the existing order. And the victims of these leaders, who are always more negative than mystical, and more materialistic than doctrinaire, are the very people whom they mislead and incite to violence, and utilize rather than serve.

In modern revolutions, and most markedly in our Spanish Revolution and in those planned by Bolshevik Communism which threaten other nations, an important and a deeply-rooted cause is a general and persistent dehumanization of the popular mind, which destroys all spiritual values, imbues the masses with materialistic and atheistic ideas, kindles in them rancour, hatred and envy and excites in them vague longings for power and the untrammelled enjoyment of material pleasures and blessings by promising them that this world shall become an earthly Paradise.

This dehumanizing process, speculating criminally with the faults and the injustices of society, is accompanied and followed by other features, which foster a violent form of irritation and impatience for the immediate accomplishment of reforms, and thrust aside methods of just and progressive evolution which constitute the chief stumbling-block of all revolutionaries, subordinating everything to the method of rapid and " direct " action, the method which revolutionary totalitarianism always favours.

First of all, we find a blind, fanatical and sentimental form of excitement directed against the supposed enemies of the people, which first invents them and then stigmatizes them, accuses them and deforms them till they resemble monsters, so as to make them in the highest degree hateful. Next comes the collective justification for homicidal and destructive action, a kind of ideological chloroforming of the conscience which blurs in the eyes of the masses any clear view which they might otherwise have of individuals and of humanity as such. It picks out its future victims and places them in social categories, under the pretext of eliminating in their persons the enemies and oppressors of the people, of liberty and justice, rolling them all, as it were, into one supreme category of universal enemy, superlatively hateful and deserving only of extermination. To do this is simply to create a myth like the figure of the *bourgeois* imagined by Socialism, or that of the Fascist superimposed upon it by Sovietism, which has learned how to exploit democratic sentimentalism just as past ages exploited the individualism of Rousseau.

Then, at long last, comes the moment for the striking of the match which is to fire all this pent-up hatred, the moment for direct action. The executives and leaders of these movements never fail to precipitate the work of the Revolution by means of an orgy of rioting which exalts popular sentimentalism and calumnifies the supposed perversity of the victim. The aim of this is to present the masses with the *fait accompli* before human nature, never wholly devoid of honesty and compassion, has overcome the effects of the Terror and made them realize that they are uselessly and unjustly sowing seeds of death and pain in people who are human beings like themselves.

" Collective crimes committed upon collective victims ", as a first-rate historian has remarked, " weigh little upon men's consciences. Priests, monks and nuns, therefore, are obvious victims, because they are anonymous, half hidden from the world by names not their own, and cut off by their vocation from family and society ties, which otherwise might be a source of protection as well as of vengeance and reprisal against their murderers."

This explains why the principal victims of revolutions are the best and the most beneficent of the people, and why the revolutionaries attack the class of person most easily picked out and at the same time the noblest and the most given to good works, the class which consists of the obscure and self-sacrificing servants of God and the ministers of His Church. These point men to a higher life, which is not of this world, but which gives this world stability and order ; for this reason they pass through life doing good to the humblest souls, to Christ's poor, to the people.

If anything is lacking in this realistic explanation of the genesis of revolutions, it is supplied by our modern revolutionaries, with their new mysticism and their new technique, their redoubtable and perfected organization, their nihilistic tactics and their use of subversive force ; these fully suffice to account for the inhuman convulsions in which Spain is now writhing and which are threatening other nations. This atheistic Bolshevik Communism has been admirably described by the Swiss writer, G. Demieville, as " the science of treason and assassination, the technique of revolution and war."

Does not Bolshevism, if we may go by the programme of the Third International, aim at establishing world-revolution by means of the implacable violence of the proletariat ? Did not Lenin coin the maxims that everything favourable to Communism is moral and that falsehood is the most effective element in Bolshevik propaganda ? Did not Stalin originate the rule of conduct which reads : " Our strength has ever consisted in our having mastered the science of knowing how to utilize the contradictions and the antagonisms of our adversaries. True Marxists have learned how to divide their enemies or to vanquish them separately, allying themselves first with one group and then with another " ? Does there not now exist, for the first time in history, an International Union of the Godless, which in 1935 alone distributed eleven million atheistic publications, written in six languages, with the object of uprooting the Faith from the heart of Christian Europe and of giving an impetus, especially in Catholic countries, to the active and implacable war against belief in God and (to use their favourite word) against " priestcraft " ? Did not the official organ of the Komintern say of Spain at the end of April 1936 : " The iron is red-hot. We must strike hard, we must strike now and we must strike boldly. The churches, the monasteries and the Jesuits must be despoiled of their wealth and discredited in the eyes of the people " ? Has it not been discovered and reported that at a Congress of the Communist International of the Godless, which met at Prague in Easter

1936, jointly with the International of the Freethinkers of Brussels, special attention was devoted to Spain ?

Neither the authors and leaders of the pseudo-Catholic opposition nor the anonymous priests who signed the anti-Pastoral will accept this biological, historical and practical explanation of the nature of the Spanish persecution and revolution, because both they themselves and the actors in the Basque drama are an example of the effect of Bolshevizing methods. Are they elated with their negative, arbitrary and casuistical line of conduct, with the part they have played as servants and lackeys of the Revolution ? If so, we must ask them to apply the methods by which they have justified the religious persecution in order to explain and justify the thousands and thousands of assassinations, still more numerous, of laymen of all classes, even of workers and peasants, and of thousands of women, adolescents and children, to say nothing of the savage demolition of houses and property of all kinds belonging to harmless and peaceful citizens, who, if their assumptions be true, must have been "aggressors of the people and armed participants in the rebellion."

Let them do this, or else let them abandon their defence of the revolutionaries : if they cannot, or do not, it will become clear that they have acted falsely in trying to maintain the Church's guilt, as though there had been a genuine clerico-military rebellion in Spain or as though the Revolution had only attacked the Army, which is able to defend itself, and had punished the unresisting Church, while respecting everything that had no connection with religion.

CHAPTER VI

WITNESS OF THE LEADERS AND ACCOMPLICES OF THE PERSECUTION

It would be useless to attempt to convince those who defend the revolutionaries with arguments of the kind just advanced, since they are blissfully ignorant of the activities of the Komintern, and consider Marxism in Spain to be a fiction created by the Anti-Marxists. More direct proofs can be furnished to them by the leaders of the persecution and the cowardly authorities who gave it their sanction, perhaps even their approval. These proofs, which they will accept as authoritative, have fortunately been provided with a gratifying generosity. They follow the usual lines of traditional hatred of religion and are of the type which everywhere and at all times has led revolutionaries to subject the Church to legal persecution and to attempt to destroy it. The evidence of these persons contributes a direct and authentic refutation of the pseudo-Catholic pamphleteers.

The President of the Catalan Government, Señor Companys, who derives such satisfaction from having been able to declare that Catalonia had set an example of peacefulness and tolerance, and had been the scene of no church-burnings during the first months of Popular Front rule, spoke as follows to a group of French Communist intellectuals:

> " There are three institutions in our midst which are the objects of violent hatred, and which have embittered the people more each year: clericalism, militarism and landlordism.[1] The movement you are now witnessing is the explosion of an immense store of wrath, an immense need for vengeance, which has been gathering force from very early times. It is this wrath which explains the impetuosity of the movement."[2]

[1] [Lit.: *latifundismo*.—Tr.]

[2] This was addressed to the correspondents of *Vu*. Cf. Bloch, op. cit., p. 32.

As Señor Azaña, President of the Spanish Republic, remarked to M. J. R. Bloch, with a " melancholy smile ", a liking for the " purifying flame " has always been a specifically Spanish taste.[1] In commenting upon this phrase, M. Bloch seems to be expressing the President's own ideas when he says: " What the people have tried to destroy, by burning churches and monasteries, is the outward and visible signs of an age-old oppression. They have flung themselves against the fortresses of a hostile power. Here their fury has stopped: everything else they have respected. Let us never weary of proclaiming this."

The military leaders are even clearer on the subject.

Andrés Nin, a leader of the Workers' Party of Marxist Unification, generally known as the POUM, declared on August 8, 1936, at a meeting held in a Barcelona theatre:

> " There are many problems in Spain and the *bourgeois* Republicans did not trouble about solving them. With regard to the problem of the Church . . . we have solved it completely by going down to its roots: we have done away with priests, churches and worship."

On March 5, 1937, José Díaz, Secretary-General of the Spanish section of the Third International, used the following words:

> " In the provinces where we hold sway, the Church no longer exists. Spain has improved greatly upon the work of the Soviets, for to-day the Church in Spain is annihilated."

Juan Peiró, one of the leaders of the C.N.T. and formerly a minister in the Valencian Government, wrote as follows:

> " The general hatred of the cassocked musketeers and of the *requetés* begotten in the shadow of the confessional, was translated into practice so literally that all priests and religious have been persecuted and exterminated simply for what they were."

[1] [Cf. p. 50, below.—Tr.]

He also makes perfectly clear the atheistic designs of the Revolution :

> " The destruction of the Church is an act of justice. . . . To destroy God, if He existed, in the heat of a revolution, when the passions of the people, inflamed with a righteous hatred, are overflowing, would be a perfectly natural and human thing to do."[1]

An Anarchist apologist of the Revolution, H. E. Kaminski, in alluding to the supposed armed priests, says in a completely natural way :

> " But all these facts, certain as they are, do not exhaust the problem. . . . It would be useless to try to soften things down. All over Spain the Revolution has raised its hand against the Church because in it the people saw the greatest obstacle to their liberation and the age-old symbol of their oppression."[2]

At almost the same time as the group of Anglican and Free Churchmen published their Report already alluded to, declaring that there was no evidence of an anti-God movement in Spain as there was in Russia, and that the Republican Government was strongly imbued with a spirit of religious tolerance, Moscow was celebrating an Anti-God Congress which was attended by 1,600 delegates from forty-six countries, its aim being to collect information about the progress accomplished in each of these countries and to perfect a plan of campaign for eradicating a belief in God throughout the world. It was here that the Spanish delegates declared that the Church in Spain was totally annihilated,[3] while Comrade Jesús Hernández, Communist Minister of Public Instruction in the Largo Caballero Government, sent the Congress a telegram worded as follows :

> " Your struggle against religion is also ours. It is our duty to make Spain a country of militant atheists. The struggle will be hard, because everywhere in this country there are great masses of reactionaries who are opposed

[1] *Perill a la reraguardia*, Mataró, 1936.
[2] *Ceux de Barcelone*, Paris, 1937, p. 192.
[3] Cf. p. 45, above.

to the absorption of Soviet culture. All Spanish schools will be transformed into Communist schools."

The Central Council of the Soviet Atheist League wrote to Señor Largo Caballero, then Prime Minister of Republican Spain, expressing its gratitude to him for his fight against religion and making him an honorary member of the Atheist League.[1]

Here is an abundance of explanations, facts and evidence which will serve as a commentary to the *Joint Letter* of the Spanish bishops which deals with the charge levelled against the Church of having defended itself against a popular movement and thus causing the deaths of its own priests.

The bishops' reply, brief, positive and full of authority and dignity, will seem to every fair-minded person to be amply justified by what has just been quoted :

"This we deny. The attack upon the churches was a sudden one, taking place in every region almost simultaneously, and coinciding with the massacre of the priests. The churches were burned because they were the Houses of God ; the clergy were sacrificed because they were the ministers of God. Proofs of this abound. The Church has not been an aggressor. . . . She succumbed where anarchical Communism prevailed—an innocent, peaceful and defenceless victim."[2]

The persecution of religion in Spain, then, has been an end in itself, a war against the Church, quite distinct from the Civil War or from any other social or political conflict, an attack prepared, directed and executed with anti-religious hatred and iconoclastic fury, which only awaited the right moment to accomplish its ideals and plans of extermination. Such will be the verdict of history.

A few words are necessary to give an idea of the horror

[1] *The Universe*, London, February 19, 1937. Cf. the pamphlet *Les Sans-Dieu en Espagne*, published by the International *Pro-Deo* Committee at Geneva. This quotes titles of books and pamphlets of the "Library of the Godless" which circulate freely in Spain. Such are: *The Holy Claws of Holy Church ; Libertinage in the Bible ; Jesus Christ, a bad man ; What a Heaven !*

[2] *Joint Letter*, p. 25.

of this persecution of religion, with which no other is comparable.

When the persecution broke out the Holy See lost no time in making continual and active protests to the Madrid Government. No satisfactory answer was ever received ; the Government took no effective step to restrain the excesses, nor did it even make any public expression of its regret for these sacrilegious acts or dissociate itself from their authors.[1]

On the other hand, the Government had no difficulty in setting up State tribunals which rapidly and implacably passed capital sentences on soldiers and civilians who had taken part in the rebellion—sentences which were immediately executed, either in the name of the law or in the form of reprisals. For the assassins, the incendiaries, the workers of obscenities, the profaners of the dead, the sacrilegious, the iconoclasts, the despoilers, the law did not exist ; for them there were no detentions, trials or condemnations. Men armed by authority to put down the military rising gave themselves up to destruction, pillage and assassination instead of to fighting. And they were allowed to do this with impunity under a pretext of legality and the preservation of order.

After the Revolution had been pursuing its triumphant course for more than a year, one single official voice was heard alluding to the persecution of religion. This was the voice of one of its ministers—a Basque—Señor Irujo, who issued a decree legalizing a new form of tolerance, a form which in the whole history of public law had never been heard of before, tolerance for clandestine worship, to grant which was, of course, to make an implicit acknowledgment of the vandalism of this nihilistic persecution. The declaration was nothing more than a confession of impotence, but it hypocritically reiterated the infamous accusation which has been rebutted above. " At the very outset of the military rebellion ", it said, " it was impossible to prevent the people from expressing their repulsion for things ecclesiastical when they saw certain priests making common cause with the Army against the people."

[1] Cf. *Osservatore Romano,* August 10, 1936.

This might seem even more difficult for the civilized world to understand than the persecution of religion itself.

We Spaniards, however, can understand it, and we can make a present of our experience to other nations in which legal laicism and anti-religious politics are preparing the way, as they did in Spain, for similar outbreaks of mob vandalism.

In every revolution authority finds itself powerless, and deserts its duties. In every persecution of religion it is the powers that be which have been responsible for the attack, and those powers then invariably proceed to complain that they are helpless and cannot restrain the vandalism of those who carry it out.

It is this that has happened in Spain.

It was in May 1931 that the burning of churches and religious houses began. When the Home Secretary, Señor Maura, a practising Catholic, attempted to repress the popular tumult and to re-establish order by having recourse to the forces of the law, the Minister of War, Don Manuel Azaña, replied: " The whole of the religious houses in Spain are not as important as the life of a single Republican."

At the end of the same year the legal persecution of the Church was initiated by an aggressively sectarian Constitution, in which, to quote the first President of the Republic, Señor Alcalá Zamora, lay hidden the germs of the Civil War. In May 1933 effect was given to this persecution by the Law of Religious Congregations and Confessions—" a law ", in the striking words of the Pope, " devoid of all justice and equity, that is to say, of the essential qualities of any law whatsoever . . . ; a law which may be called a masterpiece of iniquity, or, to use a modern expression, a record in laws directed against God and man's soul."

During the five months' rule of the Popular Front, the persecution of religion, which was a prelude to the great Revolution, assumed tremendous dimensions. And the Government imposed a policy of non-intervention—non-intervention of the forces of law and order, who might have exacerbated the temper of the masses.

During the fever of those last days of July 1936 Don Manuel Azaña, by this time President of the Republic, uttered a phrase which has since become famous. "Now at last," he declared, "the Republic has really been proclaimed!"

Early in August a group of French Communistic intellectuals was received in friendly audience at the National Palace in Madrid by President Azaña. In the middle of their conversation the President led them to a window to show them the magnificent view of the Guadarrama Mountains which the Palace affords. On the horizon was rising an enormous cloud of smoke, which, it seemed evident, was not smoke produced by cannon.

"What is that?" they asked him.

"Oh, some stupid trick!" he answered, shrugging his shoulders. "People always want to burn something. At one time they used to burn heretics; now they are burning churches. . . . We are so fond of flames—purifying flames!—in Spain."

To an apologist of the Revolution, M. J. R. Bloch, Señor Azaña once remarked: "I have never believed in intellectuals, experts and officials. I have always believed in the people, and the people have never let me down. *It is the people who are saving civilization!*"

There, in a phrase, is the whole philosophy of the Revolution and of the persecution of religion.

PART II

FLOS MARTYRUM

CHAPTER I

THE TRAGIC CONTRAST

THE War in Spain has been responsible for a most bitter and lacerating experience which for true Spaniards has been harder to bear than the War itself. I mean the abandonment into which the egoistical principle of non-intervention plunged a society overwhelmed by a materialistic, bestial and devastating revolution and the complete absence of horror which the entire world might have been expected to feel for the victims.

Though at first the War might have looked like a conflict between two political parties, it soon became clear that it was something very different. A fortnight after its outbreak it was unmasked, to even the least informed person, as in essence a combination of social nihilism and religious persecution. On the one hand it was seen to be a war of defence against a Mongolian invasion and an Anarchist reaction, inspired by a patriotism envisaging a restoration of national ideals. On the other it was the establishment of a Terror by hordes who stopped at no crime or work of destruction and set up a *régime* of tyranny which not only robbed the Government of its last claim to legitimacy but left the State without any adequate leadership.

But the world remained indifferent. And meanwhile whole classes of society were rapidly undergoing extermination. They were persecuted for their ideas and beliefs, for their family connections, for their social or professional positions, for their economic importance, for the very good deeds that they did, even for the contributions which they made to the free life of the spirit, to the common advantage of State and Nation.

From this devastating persecution nothing remained immune. Everything suffered—institutions, ideas, persons, buildings, homes, symbols, every trace of religion, culture, property, social and political relations, forms of labour, economy and government. And the attempts to destroy all these were made by organized anarchy, which would gladly have slain God, exterminated society, wiped out history, and extirpated every trace of a life which it was determined should never return.

As in every revolution, bestial instincts and elemental passions were unleashed : vengeance, hatred and envy of a personal nature found satisfaction in the administration of the law of Cain ; and pillage and crime were indulged in for the delight of doing evil for evil's sake. But in no previous revolution had these tragically normal features of disorder and violence reached a state of paroxysm nor had they been so deliberately and efficiently organized with the object of bringing about a totalitarian annihilation of society and the State. Georges Sorel would have remarked with shame that the Spanish Revolution was inspired by no single heroic sentiment ; the dialectical materialism of Marx was terribly exceeded. Only Bakunin would have been gratified to see that those two " black beasts " of his, Church and State, had been so brutally assaulted ; while Stalin persuaded himself that the fiery lava of popular fury had at last taken shape in his Asiatic mould.

And the world, accustomed to the idea that thinkers can do no wrong, has accepted the principle of extermination by means of ideas converted into crimes.

Renan, in his aristocratic retreat, meditated one day on the terrible possibility that our present-day civilization might suddenly be completely engulfed by a tremendous earthquake. It is this that has taken place in Spain—and the world has hardly noticed it ! As the Pope declared a few months after it began, " it threatens the very bases of order, culture and civilization." Or, as the Spanish bishops, direct witnesses and victims of its barbarity, wrote in their letter addressed to the whole of Christendom : " Not merely the political interests of one nation are involved, but the very foundations of social life : religion, justice, authority and the liberty of the citizen."[1]

[1] *Joint Letter*, p. 3.

Yet, despite such authoritative testimony, there has been no such universal display of horror, sympathy and pity as one might have expected.

More than 300,000 persons, who have done no wrong and who have neither thought nor written nor spoken in favour of the insurgents, have become victims of the Proletarian Revolution. As to those who have survived, the sum total of their burdens—family afflictions, spoliation, misery, constant terror—has indescribably increased the tragedy of the War. The homes that have been destroyed, the estates that have been pillaged would represent, if they could all be put together, whole cities destroyed by the Revolution without reference to military exigences but simply out of nihilistic fervour.

It is difficult, too, to exaggerate the immense losses which have been suffered by history, art and thought through the destruction of so great a part of Spain's cultural heritage. Nor has any such protest been heard against this vandalism as resounded through Europe at the time of the bombardment of Rheims Cathedral and the burning of the Louvain Library.

It is true that heroic work has been done to save the lives of potential victims by Embassies, Legations and Consulates —heroic both because of the loftiness of their aim, which they often successfully accomplished, and also because of the opposition raised to it by the revolutionaries and the Madrid Government, though the right of asylum had always been considered one of the few sacred and inviolable principles which persisted in civilized communities.[1]

Despite all the efforts of jurists and diplomats, despite the magnificent and determined attempts of the Spanish-American governments, both in Madrid and in Geneva, that disciple of Moscow Alvarez del Vayo succeeded in persuading the League of Nations to degrade itself further by failing to defend the right of asylum possessed by the foreign legations in Spain, where thousands of human beings were sacrificed

[1] Cf. the testimony of the Baron de Borchgrave, of the Belgian Legation in Spain, published in the *Catholic Herald* of February 5, 1937, and that of Miguel Pérez Ferrero, in *Drapeau de France* (Paris, Sorlot), the preface to which is dated January 28, 1938.

to the insatiable demands of those who aimed at exterminating civilization.

Nowhere in the high places of intellect and authority has there been any sign of a proper sensitiveness, either to the intense human suffering of crucified Spain or to the rights of the spirit, which to an extent unparalleled in history have been trampled underfoot by the red beast of Revolution.

CHAPTER II

THE VICTIMS' REPLY

On the contrary, by strange processes of intellectual perversion, many whom one would have expected to have sympathized with the victims of the persecution and to have defended the interests of society, have taken the side of the persecutors and championed their inhuman cause with a zeal that would have been better expended upon those who are upholding order and civilization. Luigi Sturzo, for example, completely misunderstanding the situation and taking a biased view of the facts, has spoken of the Spanish people as though they were simply a religious community being persecuted as such, implied that they have been treated no more harshly than were the early Christians by the Roman emperors, and reproached them for not having imitated these martyrs by practising the principle of non-resistance to evil and accepting the supreme self-sacrifice.[1]

Many of the innumerable twentieth-century martyrs of whom the Spanish people to-day are so justly proud have indeed done this, and the sublimity of their heroism is nowhere surpassed in the entire records of primitive Christian martyrology. But there is a vast difference between strictly individual and spiritual persecution and a persecution which threatens the most essential foundations of human society. The duty of the early Christians was to witness to their Faith, remain loyal to their God and insist upon the Christian's right to freedom of conscience in the future. Though citizens of the Roman Empire, they could not have been expected to defend its institutions, for these were not theirs and had not as yet been christianized. The order, culture and civilization of twentieth-century Spain, on the

[1] " Politique d'abord ? Non ! Morale d'abord." (*L'Aube*, September 6, 1936.) " Le droit de révolte et ses limites." (*Vie intellectuelle*, October 25, 1937.)

other hand, were Christian in their origins and history; and it was these for which Christians rightly fought, since they were in danger of disappearing under the repeated attacks made upon their very human and social foundation by the godless and the enemies of humanity.

Who can deny to a society which finds itself in such straits the right—and the Christian right—to defend by force institutions the preservation of which depends upon a social and political order imposed where necessary by armed force? The principle of non-resistance to evil has not been, and can never be, a norm of conduct in temporal societies.[1]

Yet M. Jacques Maritain continues to display the spectre of clerical imprudence as a cause of the paroxysm of anti-religious fury in question. He is shocked that a Spanish religious and professor should have spoken of the anti-Communist campaign as a Holy War and a Crusade. In order to meet any quibbling objection about his confusing spiritual issues with temporal, he then constructs a complicated case, according to which it appears that the Popular Front's militiamen are also engaged in a Holy War, and that one must speak with equal respect of the heroic sacrifice made by both groups of combatants.

We have ourselves never despised those who, mistaken as they may be, are nobly defending their ideals and sacrificing their very lives for them. We sympathize, in a spirit of true Christian love, with all the victims of perverse systems, dazzled by corrupt agents with the illusions of modern Utopian mysticism and thus led to take part in revolutionary movements at the cost of their own blood. We will not deny that at the beginning of the Revolution a by no means negligible

[1] Pius XI's Encyclical (March 28, 1937) on the religious situation in Mexico expounds the moral principles governing the lawfulness of a rising against those who use public power in order to plunge a nation into ruin and thus destroy the very foundations of authority. The first author to treat in detail of the position in Spain and to discuss, with exceptional competence, the lawfulness of the Nationalist movement against a tyrannical Government, was Dr. Enrique Pla y Deniel, Bishop of Salamanca, in his pastoral of September 30, 1936, entitled "The Two Cities." His teaching was utilized and amplified by the Spanish Bishops in their *Joint Letter* of July 1937. Cf. also P. I. Menéndez Raigada, O.P.: *La Guerra nacional española ante la Moral y el Derecho* (Salamanca, 1937); Louis Le Fur: *La Guerre d'Espagne et le droit* (Paris, 1938); and Dr. Enrique Pla y Deniel: *Pío XI y España* (Salamanca, 1938).

number of political and social idealists were drawn into the ranks of the Government's militia. But who can fairly place on one and the same footing the cause of the Revolution (which is not the cause of anti-Fascism), in which all those who fight for it must in some degree be held responsible for the excesses of the Anarcho-Marxists and their attacks upon the fundamentals of civilization, and the cause of the Nationalists, which is not the cause of Italy and Germany, but which stands for the defence of civilization, shoulder to shoulder with the victims of a society which these criminal dynamite-heroes have attempted to terrorize and subdue?

It will be observed that the Pope and the Spanish bishops do not as a rule, in their solemn official utterances, use the terms "holy war" and "crusade" when referring to what the Pope has repeatedly described as the "great combat" against atheistic and Bolshevik Communism. But, when one considers the grandeur of the ideals and the motives which have inspired the great anti-Communist combat to which the whole world is called and in the cause of which Spain has made a unique sacrifice for the sake of all other nations, is it surprising that such terms should rise unbidden to many lips, not so much because of sporadic incidents connected with the combat as because of its noble objective? Class strife, said the Pope in his Encyclical on Communism, with the hatred and destruction which it implies, is taking on the aspect of a crusade for the progress of humanity. Why, then, in the name of reason and justice, should it be wrong to give the same name to the great spiritual and social enterprise which the Church is carrying on against the godless and against Marxist anti-civilization? Why should not the name be used (though, of course, in a less literal sense) of a national rising which in its heroic defence of its ideals unites all sections of Christendom, and, indeed, of humanity? If, as M. Maritain himself admits, Don John of Austria at Lepanto, and Sobïeski at the gates of Vienna, are the last representatives of the mediæval Holy War against an Islam which threatened Christian Europe, we see no reason why civilization should refuse the title of crusade to the movement of liberation inaugurated by National and Catholic Spain against the invasion of Moscow.

At the very beginning of the movement the learned Bishop of Salamanca, Dr. Pla y Deniel, in the Pastoral entitled "The Two Cities" already referred to, states his conclusions as follows:

> "Although it is true that the present struggle presents the external appearance of a civil war, it is in reality a crusade. It was a rising which aimed, not at overthrowing order but at restoring it. A struggle, in fact, of order against anarchy, the objects of which were to establish a government which Communism would have dissolved, and to defend Christian civilization and its fundamental elements—religion, the Motherland and the family—against those who either know not God or reject Him and against those who own no country but (to use the apt phrase of a Christian poet) are dependent upon the charity of the world."

An outstanding Italian writer, P. Enrico Rosa, well aware of the objections that have been raised to the use of the word "crusade", goes so far, in commenting on the Spanish Bishops' *Joint Letter*, as to say:

> "It is something more than a Crusade; it is a campaign against foreign subvertors of civilization and common malefactors, men far worse than the Mohammedans and the Moors. In those who are at present invading Spain the perversion of the apostate and the ingenuity of modern humanity are united with energy and hatred."[1]

But M. Maritain has accepted neither the guidance offered by Pius XI to all who are looking at the Spanish question from the standpoint of Catholicism, nor the judgment of the Bishops' *Joint Letter*. He declines to take sides. "To refuse to support Salamanca", he remarks, "is not to support Valencia."[2] But when one is faced with such transcendental facts as the Great War or the present tragedy of Spain, an

[1] "Il Martirio della Spagna," in *La Civiltà Cattolica*, September 1937, p. 486.
[2] Cf. preface to A. Mendizábal: *Aux Origines d'une Tragédie*, Paris, 1937, originally published in the *Nouvelle Revue Française* for July 1, 1937. On this preface see also Vice-Admiral H. Joubert: *La Guerre d'Espagne et le Catholicisme*.

attitude of contemplative indifference or of evasive criticism is wholly unacceptable. One cannot but be a belligerent—and one's belligerency is rooted in a position of inescapable humane and Christian solidarity, with ideals which one knows to be right.

This was the attitude taken by an impressive number of French intellectuals in their "Manifesto to the intellectuals of Spain", which testifies to the strength of the ties uniting those who represent culture and intellect in both countries. This should also have been the decisive attitude taken by those who are united by the still closer bonds of Catholic faith and thought.

Unhappily, the small but vocal group of Catholics who have declared their antagonism to the war against Communism in Spain have acted very differently. They seem to have found inspiration against the forces of evil in a kind of evangelical integralism. When it is pointed out to them that they find it conveniently easy to forget the attempts which have been made to exterminate the Church in Spain, they reply that these criminal acts have been solemnly denounced by the Holy See, and that many opponents of the Nationalists have from the beginning deprecated them with all possible emphasis,[1] and so they persist in their "inexplicable attitude of mistrust towards the defenders of order and humanity, to say nothing of religion and morality, among the nations."[2]

But their very explanations and their determination to assign responsibility in equal measure to the two opposing forces, only emphasize the weighing-down of the balance on one side. It is impossible to disguise the fact that two features dominate the Spanish tragedy: a terrible social revolution which aims at nothing less than extermination and an implacable campaign of religious persecution. It is impossible to excuse, or even to give a veneer of respectability to the heroes of the Spanish Terror, or to those who greeted the rising of Red Spain with the words "*Russia for ever!*"—and, from their point of view, rightly so, since Soviet Russia

[1] Eg. Francisque Gay: *Dans les flammes et dans le sang*. Cf. Maritain's preface, op. cit., p. 44. P. I. Menéndez Raigada, O.P., has replied effectively to M. Maritain's criticisms in *Ciencia Tomista*, 1937, Nos. 5–6.

[2] *La Civiltà Cattolica*, September 18, 1937.

is committed to the enterprise of stirring up a universal revolution, of which the Spanish Revolution is only the initial stage.

Those who bolster up these crimes have not the courage to proclaim to the world, like Paul Claudel, the awfulness, and yet the greatness, of the martyrdom of the sixteen thousand priests :

> " Seize mille prêtres ! le contingent d'un seul coup et le ciel en un seul coup de flamme colonisé ! "[1]

They will not, like him, declare : " I am for Spain !—for Spain ! "

> " En cette heure de ton crucifiement, sainte Espagne, en ce jour, sœur Espagne, qui est ton jour."[2]

They prefer to take up an attitude which the always temperate P. Enrico Rosa (already quoted) has described as one which " attenuates or excuses revolutionaries who are among the most brutal, savage and sanguinary that history has known ". They would have done better to have defended the revolutionaries' innocent victim, the Church, whose future protection they claim and whose highest interests they invoke as the sole and spiritual origin of what we must describe as their " political theology " of excusing revolution.

As the *Osservatore Romano* remarked, with bitter truth, in a striking article entitled " The Two Wars " (October 21, 1937) :

> " No one has taken into account the consideration which ought to be outside and above all controversy, since it has to do with universality of faith and thought : no one has paid any attention to the sanguinary aggression and incendiarism which Spain has suffered for the sake of religion.

[1] " Aux Martyrs espagnols," Claudel's verse preface to Juan Estelrich's *La Persécution religieuse en Espagne* (Paris, Plon, 1937), a book which has done much to make the truth about the persecution widely known. In making this quotation, we have naturally followed the original text, but it should be noted that the poet's figure of sixteen thousand is not to be found in documented studies of the Revolution. A more reliable and a later source is the Spanish Bishops' *Joint Letter*.

[2] Claudel : op. cit.

"Men have succoured refugees, defended the defenceless and published all kinds of polemic concerning the cruelty of war waged on land and sea and in the air. But no one has troubled to defend the most defenceless victim of all, the victim of whom the greatest sacrifices have been demanded, who could never become a refugee because it was her duty to remain at her post even unto death."

And some, led away by sectarianism or political passion, or (less excusably) from sheer love of inopportune criticism, have propagated and helped to keep alive the completely unjustifiable legend that the recent persecution of the Church has been a kind of punishment or reprisal inflicted by a neglected and oppressed people, and that its motive has been anti-clerical fury rather than hatred of God and of religion.

The fact that "brother is killing brother", to quote the phrase with which, soon after the outbreak of war, the Pope lamented its horrors, does not cease to torture all who witness it, suffer through it or even take part in it. None would deny that the effects of even the most just and holy war are terrible and inhuman, or that civil war, which destroys the brotherly love that should characterize compatriots and fellow Christians, is the most terrible and the most to be deprecated of all. This we recognize only too well, with hearts wellnigh broken. None more earnestly than Spaniards, who are familiar with all the grievous details of this tragedy, desire their speedy termination by a victory and a peace that shall bring both reparation and justice.

But, though we have been witnesses and victims of the devastation, sacrilege and slaughter of the Revolution, and have felt, as it were, each one of us in himself, the anguish caused by the mortal wounds which our country has suffered, we have not felt able to resign ourselves to a collective acceptance of death or to restrict ourselves to lamenting the sufferings of our fellow countrymen on the one side of the line or on the other. Nor do we indulge in the furious language of polemists who call down from Heaven a consuming fire for the extermination of their enemy, as did the Sons of Thunder in the days of old. No: unjustly persecuted and sacrificed though we have been, our first thought is of forgiveness. We beseech God with all our hearts that the days of our testing may be shortened, and we convert into intercessory oblations the sacrifice of the lives of those near and dear to us, the seizure of property necessary to our livelihood, the ruin of institutions which we have loved: above all, the open and incurable wound in the body of the nation, the destruction of that heritage which we have received from our fathers and which has come down to us through generations and even centuries.

Yet all this vast body of intercession has not sufficed to end the War—not even the intercession of the noble army of our Martyrs, who even in the moments of their agony have pardoned and blessed their murderers and witnessed to the glory of God.

The truth is that peace cannot come in Spain until the Revolution is effectively and completely vanquished both in its works and as to its spirit.

These lines will suffice to set out the problem as it affects Spain. But there is another aspect of it—an aspect of universal transcendence, to be viewed on the lofty plane of the philosophy of history, where those of our detractors who look on calmly at our sorrows delight to seat themselves. Neither we Spaniards, who are suffering from the effects of this war in our souls and bodies, nor those abroad who expect universal blessings to proceed from its happy issue, can forget the words of the Pope, the witness of the Spanish Bishops, and the echoes of both to be found in letters written by the Cardinals-Archbishops of Paris, Malines and Westminster. Here we have reflections of the mentalities of Christian countries and peoples very different from Spain and the Spanish people. Nor must we forget how within Spain itself, at the very beginning of the War, that great mystic and great independent, Miguel de Unamuno, summed up the situation:

> "Before all else we must save Western Christian civilization from barbarism."[1]

[1] See *Le Matin*, September 11, 1936.

Let us not forget such truths as these :

" To a world which has been completely penetrated, overwhelmed, turned upside down by subversive propaganda, in particular to a Europe at present so sorely agitated and shaken, the tragic happenings in Spain announce once more the disastrous nature of the extremes which threaten all the foundations of order, culture and civilization."[1]

" The Civil War, so terrible in itself, has now been exacerbated by a war of religion. Throughout the territory in which Communism reigns there has been an infernal orgy : churches and religious houses have been burned ; bishops, priests, monks and nuns have been assassinated ; persons and things representative of the Catholic religion have been exterminated without mercy. Let us bow our heads with respect before these noble victims of a Satanic hatred of the name of Christian, since we are justified in believing that they have gained the palm of martyrdom in the strictest and highest sense. This War, then, has taken on the character of a death-struggle between atheistic and materialistic Communism and the Christian civilization of our Western States."[2]

" The anti-God forces have resolved to make Spain the strategic centre of a world revolution against the very foundations of the civilized society of Europe. It is a question of a struggle between Christian civilization and the so-called civilization of Sovietic atheism."[3]

" What is in question in this war is the future of the Catholic Church and of the civilization which she has founded. If to-day Spain offers the example of a sacrifice unique in history it is because the enemies of God chose her as the first stage in their work of destruction."[4]

" We cannot do other than desire the triumph in Spain of what at present stands for civilization against barbarism,

[1] Pius XI : *Allocution of September* 14, 1936.

[2] *Collective Pastoral of the Belgian Episcopate,* December, 1936 ; *Letter of Cardinal Van Roey, Archbishop of Malines, to the Spanish Episcopate,* January 16, 1938.

[3] *Reply of Cardinal Hinsley, Archbishop of Westminster, to Cardinal Gomá,* September, 1937.

[4] *Reply of Cardinal Verdier to Cardinal Gomá,* September, 1937.

for order and justice against violence, for tradition against destruction, and for the safety of the individual against the most arbitrary acts."[1]

Such noble and convincing words as these ought surely to have put an end to the qualms of those whom Claudel strikingly describes as " tous ces lâches et tous ces hésitants " and " tous ces pauvres douteurs de doutes ". But these critics of National Spain, with their fallacious equanimity and their tendentious humanitarianism, were unmoved by them. The only horrors of the War which they anathematized were those which gave them a handle against the Nationalists ; they thought nothing of the injustice and bitter grief into which hundreds of thousands of innocent victims were plunged by the Revolution.

One of the most deplorable of their manifestations was the following unhappy dialogue which occurs in an article by François Mauriac.[2] In this article the eminent academician expresses his disapproval of the letters written by foreign Bishops in support of the *Joint Letter* of the Spanish Bishops and makes a flank attack on their attitude of marked sympathy with National and Catholic Spain. The dialogue runs thus :

> " Which do you think excite the greater pity in the heart of God—those who were beheaded or otherwise executed by enraged multitudes and by the leaders of the Popular Front, or the victims of bombardments planned and executed with the utmost coldness, devoid of all emotions, either of pleasure or of hatred, by foreign mercenaries ? "
>
> " Who knows ? Perhaps the saints could tell us. . . ."
>
> " Ah ! If a voice were suddenly heard—one voice, just one. . . ."
>
> " But the saints no longer speak."

Well, this particular voice may not have been heard—because those it addressed were not listening for it. But a reply was made to M. Mauriac, asking what exactly he

[1] *Manifesto of the French intellectuals*, December, 1937.
[2] *Le Figaro*, October 13, 1937.

means by invoking this voice, which would need to make itself heard above the noisy vituperations of militant atheists, of infuriated Anarchists and of wild Bolsheviks, and which he would presumably expect to plead for leniency with these parties. Would he seriously propose that Spanish citizens and the Spanish army should abandon the defence of their religion and their country—to say nothing of their allies, who have no desire for Bolshevik victories in the Mediterranean ?

We ourselves are happy to present M. Mauriac with two replies : that of the Saints whose innocent blood cries out from the pages of our Spanish martyrology and whose voice he will be able to hear, if he is so inclined, in our narrative ; and another, speaking with simpler accents, but giving a straightforward and dignified answer to the crooked questions of the revolutionaries. Let us hear this second voice now.

In November 1936 the Department of Propaganda of the autonomous Government of Catalonia sent the *Osservatore Romano* some photographs depicting school-children and tiny inmates of orphanages who had been victims of the Madrid bombardments. The *Osservatore*, in acknowledging the photographs, naturally replied that it had always deplored the tragic consequences of aerial bombardment, and then added that it would be very grateful if the Catalan Government " would supplement the information it had sent by forwarding photographs of the bodies of priests, monks and nuns who had been assassinated, deliberately and in cold blood, by the heroic defenders of freedom."[1]

But the most strident note to be struck is that of M. Georges Bernanos in his book *Les Grands Cimetières sous la lune.*[2] M. Bernanos claims to have been the witness of a " white terror " in Majorca, where he lived, and on this claim he bases sweeping judgements upon the policy of the Hierarchy and the reform of the Catholic spirit. No person

[1] It is reported that the Propaganda Department replied by sending a photograph said to have been found in the house of an aristocrat, the Conde de Vallellano, in which five persons in monks' dress are standing, with cocked rifles or pistols, round a machine-gun, which forms the centre of the composition. But this is really too good to be credible !

[2] Paris, 1938. [An English version of this book has recently been published under the title *Diary of My Times.*—Tr.]

or institution escapes his condemnation— not even the serene figure of Pius XI, whose voice will go down to history as that of an intrepid defender of truth and righteousness against both Cæsarean and demagogic oppression. The Church, we are told, is tottering, Christianity is engulfed, saintliness is ineffective, the Pontificate is no longer the supreme guide of the modern world, and General Compromise is the new and universally revered leader, sterilizing Christian energy and subordinating all social and spiritual values to injustice and force. The Church feeds upon others and herself feeds nobody ; the picture M. Bernanos draws of her is a gloomy one : she has not, to him, a single spark of greatness.

The account which he gives of his own country is depressing enough, but his ideas on Spain are distorted by passion and completely devoid of courtesy. The episcopate could hardly be attacked more violently. General Franco is portrayed as a kind of episcopal general and the Bishops side with him because he protects them and avenges their dead. Their motives are interpreted, in terms of disrespect and effrontery, as materialistic and Machiavellian. They are supposed, before the War, to have controlled elections and political power ; they are the authors of the Crusade, which is described as a farce ; Cardinal Gomá is a crafty leader who gave his blessing to the movement because it had received the support of the Army. Not a word is said of the horrors of the Revolution or of the noble roll of Catholic martyrs.

As to the author's accusations against the episcopate, one observation will suffice. During the entire life of the Republic the attitude maintained by the Spanish episcopate was exemplary—an attitude of apostolic courage and prudence. During the War, all its actions have been dictated by an intense zeal for the highest interests of the Church and of Spain and by a profound realism. There have never been any political leaders among the Spanish Bishops nor are there any military leaders among them to-day. They acted then, as they are acting now, *nec temere nec timide*, and they may confidently await the judgement upon them of history.

One further point. Never, during the stern testing of the last seven years, has the Holy Father failed to encourage the Spanish Hierarchy;[1] on the other hand, despite the horrors of war which both the Holy See and the Bishops have done their utmost to mitigate, there has been witnessed in the "New Spain" a powerful uprising of the religious consciousness. Thus the Pope was able to assure General Franco of his happiness "at perceiving in his message of homage the vibration of the authentic voice of Catholic Spain,"[2] while the Hierarchy, completely independent and enjoying the respect of the nation, directed the nation's allegiance, by means of Cardinal Gomá's vigorous phraseology, to the true and only Catholicism, that of the Roman obedience centred in the Vatican.[3]

[1] Cf. the letter from Cardinal Pacelli to Cardinal Gomá (March 5, 1938).
[2] Telegram on the canonization of San Salvador de Horta, April 18, 1938.
[3] *Pío XI y España* (Pastoral of January 28, 1938).

CHAPTER III

VINDICATION OF THE MARTYRS

THE sufferings of the soul of Spain do not end here. Not only has the Revolution had its victims, but these victims have not even been rendered the universal homage of an understanding and a disinterested compassion: the glory of martyred Spain, or the extent of that glory, is underestimated or unknown altogether. And it has been left to a few misguided priests, with their deadly ideas on " neutrality ", to set up the INRI over the infamous cross on which Spain's Christian and patriotic ideals have been left to perish. With an incredible complacency the authors of the anti-Pastoral already referred to have repeated to the Spanish Bishops the story that crowds have been fired upon from churches, and in the course of their polemic have maintained that " the priests who have been killed are not martyrs, nor is the burning of the churches any proof of hatred of religion : both these constitute the natural defence of the people against its aggressors." " If ", they conclude, " there have been any martyrs on the one side—a very doubtful question, which needs proof—there are thousands of heroes on the other who are sacrificing their lives for the freedom and independence of their country."

Contrast with these words those of Pius XI on the religious persecution in Spain. Pius XI, better qualified than these priests to judge the true value of the evidence for martyrdom, has proclaimed the glory of our martyrs in the fullest and most sacred sense of that most glorious word. In uttering words of comfort to those shipwrecked ones on the seas of persecution who had come into the presence of the Father of Christendom, he left no doubt on this point. Those whom he received had been " despoiled and stripped of everything, persecuted and sought out by their would-be murderers, in cities and villages, in the dwellings of men and in the solitude of the mountains, exactly as were the first martyrs, whom the Apostle contemplated with such fullness of admiration that he proclaimed to the world those proud and splendid words: 'Of whom the world was not worthy.'" The Pope goes on to describe his joy and theirs, that, like the first apostles, they should have been counted worthy to suffer for the name of Jesus, and to declare the depth of his happiness and theirs that they should have been covered with scorn, and have suffered for Jesus' name, because they were Christians.

Following such an example, we can hardly be reproached if, after discovering the true nature of the religious persecution, we contemplate our martyrs with all humility and reverence and become, subject always to the definitive judgement of the Holy See, *Cultores Martyrum* of the New Spain.

Such is the quiet but adequate answer which we shall make to detractors of the Church, and of Spain.

Incomparable is the difference between the heroes of the Revolution and the martyrs of the faith—that great legion of the Church's children, who suffered death without resisting their murderers in the most terrible persecution which in one single nation has ever been seen.

The splendid art of José María Sert, so much of which was destroyed by mobs in Vich Cathedral, has had a new birth in the Pontifical Pavilion of the Paris Exhibition of 1937. And to Sert it has been given to put first into plastic form a vision of the once crucified Christ descending from Heaven to receive into glory the ever-increasing legion of our martyrs, whom Saint Teresa, presents to Him as they come.

Only when the *Flos Martyrum* of the new Spain comes to be written will the appropriateness of this representation become fully manifest. Already data and narratives are being collected by authorities and subjected to a rigorous examination. On these we shall draw in the pages which follow, outlining the main events of our terrible story, and neither selecting only the most extreme and most repugnant incidents of the persecution nor making any attempt, as has so often been done by journalists, to give the facts a dramatic colour. We have made all the efforts in our power to verify the facts which we report, especially those relating to Catalonia, which we have had the opportunity of testing more thoroughly than the rest. Should any later corrections become necessary we shall be very glad to incorporate them in this book. On our own side we have corrected a number of statements made by earlier writers which have been found to be inexact, without naming their authors; in cases where the correctness of earlier reports, sometimes referring to well-known persons and incidents, seemed doubtful, we have said nothing.

It should be emphasized that our intention is not so much to record the horrors of the persecution of religion in Spain as to tell of the glory of the Spanish martyrs and to underline the innumerable examples of abnegation and spirituality given both by themselves and by their associates and relatives. The standpoint from which we write, and our fundamental position throughout, may be best described in words used by the *Osservatore Romano* on October 20, 1937, in the course of a commentary on the Spanish Bishops' *Joint Letter*:

"On the one hand there are the Reds; on the other, the Catholic Church and the Nationalists. . . . Between the two social and political fields lies the field of religion. Between the two sides which are striving for the life of a nation is God striving for the life of the Faith. Standing outside the two armed parties is the Church—no combatant, but a martyr."

CHAPTER IV

GENERAL CHARACTERISTICS OF THE PERSECUTION

IN an earlier chapter, dealing with the origins of the persecution of religion, we have already given a detailed explanation of its causes and of the general traits which characterized it from the first moments of its outbreak. It has been nothing less than a paroxysm of Satanic fury, organized, prepared and kept alive with brutal efficiency. The main lines of its attack have shown it to be systematically and skilfully carried out on totalitarian lines, though it is true that it has also been characterized by unrehearsed episodes of irresponsible bestiality or of emotional reaction, of a type which recurs in all revolutions.

Throughout the territory of the Red zone the persecution of religion began at once to show itself in its true and brutal colours. It is clear from the first of the *Official Reports* of which the publication by the National Government has begun[1] that the mad passion of the persecutors and revolutionaries has been particularly violent in the south and centre of Spain and along the eastern seaboard : here, too, vandalism in matters of religious art has been peculiarly severe. But it is perhaps in Catalonia, above all, for reasons already explained, that the concordance of plan, methods and aims stands out most clearly.

We must take into account all these diverse factors and characteristics of the persecution if we are to attempt so much as the briefest synthesis of it in which the facts to be recorded will have a representative, not merely a local or anecdotic, value and will illumine the broad perspectives of a devastated area, geographically of a considerable extent,

[1] Four volumes of these reports have been issued to date. See also the full report published by Charles Ledré under the title, *Les Crimes du Front Populaire en Espagne.*

over the whole of which death and destruction have been wrought by this inconceivable and insatiable Reign of Terror. Isolated narratives and descriptions torn from their context will, of course, suffice to shock the serenest minds, but only a bird's-eye view of the phenomenon considered as a whole can convey anything like the tragic emotion felt by the victims of this diabolic volcanic eruption which has engulfed centuries of history and decapitated as it were an entire society—an eruption which, though it began yesterday, is still active to-day.

It is this bird's-eye view which foreigners, quite naturally, find it difficult to obtain ; yet it is only when they have participated in the tragic emotion felt by Spaniards that they can begin to understand the true nature of the Spanish tragedy itself, and the steadfast determination to restore the glories of Spain which this has inspired. None, perhaps, have felt its full force—none will bear the marks of it in their hearts for ever—save those Spaniards who, with the burning of their churches and the murder of their loved ones searing their memory, have accomplished the perilous flight from their own land, and, crossing the frontier, have found themselves once more in a free and civilized Christian country, with not only churches in its towns and villages, but even the familiar wayside crosses set on its roads. At last, after so long a period in which they have been forced to say their prayers in hiding, in imminent peril of death, they can join freely with the faithful in worshipping God in safety, hear Mass as of old, and have once more before them the Eternal Word present on the Altar. How indescribable is their emotion as they realize that they have passed from death unto life ! Only this tragic yet comforting contrast can give the measure of the disaster ; and it is this which our brethren in countries which have not yet suffered need to experience before they can understand. Let them look at the Spanish cataclysm and then imagine their own national inheritance destroyed, as it were, in the twinkling of an eye—in a week of inhuman extermination and diabolic vandalism—as ours has been. In that way alone can they learn the true lesson of love.

We invite our readers in other countries, as they read these pages, to make some such effort of the imagination as this which will be to their advantage and to our encouragement. It is well that we should all learn to know evil, and still more to appreciate good; and God has indeed brought good out of evil through the sacrifice of the lives of our martyrs, through their exemplary deaths and through the conduct of those who have survived them, sanctified as they have been by the trial of suffering for God and for their country.

CHAPTER V

THE EXTINCTION OF CATHOLIC WORSHIP

THE first aspect of the persecution of religion in Spain which impresses those who have lived through it, which after two years of civil war stands out above all others, and which will remain in the memory even after the long and arduous period of restoration which must come when the War is over is the determination of the revolutionaries to destroy all visible signs of Catholic worship as part of the nation's social life. The Revolution flung itself brutally upon the churches, and upon the Church itself, like the avalanche of a vandalism intent upon annihilating its principal enemy and destroying that enemy's dwelling.

The Bishops, in their *Joint Letter*, calculate—and they are certainly not exaggerating—that over twenty thousand churches and chapels have been destroyed or completely plundered, and this in hardly more than half the total area of Spain, where alone the revolutionaries gained the day.

In the region of Catalonia, with its 2,400,000 inhabitants, its eight diocesan capitals and its numerous small towns of between fifteen and sixty thousand inhabitants, with its 2050 parishes, its 900 religious houses and its hermitages and sanctuaries in almost every town and village—in Catalonia alone the number of churches so treated is over four thousand.

In Barcelona the incendiaries and the plunderers spared the Cathedral, together with the parish church of SS. Justo and Pastor, the church of San Severo and that of the Oratory of St. Philip Neri, which are near the headquarters of the autonomous Catalan Government. No less than two hundred and twenty churches and public chapels of a considerable size, many of them monuments of history and art, have been burned and pillaged, fifty-seven of these being parish churches. Most of them met their fate during the first forty-eight hours of the Revolution. In the large towns of Catalonia, as many as eight, ten and fourteen churches were burned in a single night ; at Vich many more were burned in broad daylight. In the whole of Catalonia only a few churches, whose roots are deeply embedded in the history of religion and art, escaped destruction : such were Tarragona Cathedral and the Sanctuary of Montserrat.

It should be noted that the churches had no real security against destruction, either during the period of so-called "anarchistic order" (a cynical phrase which we owe to J. R. Bloch) or during the "governmental order" which marked the second stage of the Revolution. Neither the discipline of the front line nor that of the militias in the rearguard could protect them. At all times and in all places the rule of vandalism was supreme. One has only to remember the descriptions of the retreat of the Reds in the majority of the towns from which they were driven by Nationalist advances. Or there is the most recent and therefore most representative case of Teruel. During the brief period of Red rule in that city, the churches were destroyed with methodical refinement ; in the Cathedral only one altar (stripped of its ornaments) remained, and only one reredos ; in the other churches there was not even so much as this. When the General made his triumphal entry into the Cathedral, a priest led the rejoicings of the people in a *Te Deum*—and the crucifix set up on that occasion was the only one that could be found intact among the ruins. In the course of those few days of Red rule in Teruel, no less than twenty-seven priests were assassinated.

This extinction of visible worship has been an example of organized totalitarianism which implied not only the devastation of the churches, but the destruction of all articles used in worship, of religious symbols and of everything that represents the idea of God and the Christian idea of redemption.

Let us see how this religious nihilism was accomplished.

The teams of iconoclasts began their work upon the parish churches (without forgetting the presbyteries) ; they then attacked the other churches and the monasteries and convents—in the large towns first of all, then in the smaller towns and in the villages. Some of these groups of incendiaries, in their zeal, even climbed mountains and spent four or five hours making the ascent of heights like that of Tagamanent, in order to set fire to the modest hermitages which have been erected on their summits.

The second stage of the work of destruction consisted in the investigation by special groups of the most remote and solitary villages in which difficulties of communication, the very insignificance of the hamlets and the complete absence of revolutionary atmosphere had left churches and chapels immune.

Occasionally these buildings escaped destruction for other reasons: sometimes they were required for secular purposes; sometimes, for local reasons, the Revolutionary Committees thought it best to leave them; sometimes municipal authorities begged for their preservation as monuments of art. On these occasions the usual procedure was to drag out of the churches everything that could be moved—altars, statues, ornaments, sacred vessels—and make a bonfire of them.

The very thought of this vast constellation of almost simultaneously burning churches created with such surprising rapidity over so wide an area should be sufficient to shock the most indifferent and to prove that the extinction of public worship was the Revolution's primary aim.

Once they were let loose in the churches, the iconoclasts' first objective was the Tabernacle; their next, the Altar; after that, the Crucifix; finally, their instructions would be that they were to set fire to all ornaments, images, reredoses and whatever else they might find.

Their predilection for the destruction of altar-stones was very marked. One most reliable witness describes how he left his hiding-place in a forest for a neighbouring hermitage to say Mass at one of its altars. When he reached this, he discovered, not only that all three of its altar-stones had been destroyed, but that they had been carefully smashed into the smallest fragments so that they could never again be used. A landed proprietor who had a private oratory in his house was ordered by a group of men who came to destroy it to give up the altar-stone, which he had hidden, upon pain of death. In another village the leader of the incendiaries ordered his gang to "smash that stone: they won't be able to say their Masses without it."[1]

Attempts have been made to minimize or deny the deliberateness of the attacks upon the churches: they have been described as the spontaneous acts of a noisy, popular type of anti-clericalism because they were to a very large extent the work of youths. But again and again police were standing by, their silence giving consent. And it is even more to the point that there were always men of maturer years in the background, working at the orders of committees located either on the spot or at some distance. Let us take one typical case. In the district of Bajo Empurdán, in the province of Gerona, the Committees of La Bisbal and Palafrugell sent out lorry-loads of incendiaries, these being youths of about twenty, who were paid at the rate of ten pesetas a day. The La Bisbal Committee was quite generous to the churches: only twenty-nine were profaned, and the bonfires of church furniture and articles used in Divine worship were for the most part lit outside the buildings. But the mercenaries employed by the Palafrugell Committee set fire to seventeen churches, the incendiarism taking place in the interiors of the buildings themselves: the orders given here had been much more strict and severe.

Then there was another great task of extermination—the attack, planned on the largest scale ever known in history, upon individual liberty: the complete extirpation of all religious articles and symbols, whether found on public thoroughfares, on private property, in the homes of citizens or upon their very persons.

Little chapels built on country estates, family oratories installed in private houses, shrines erected in honour of the Saints in village streets or humble homes, Stations of the Cross, monumental crosses set up long ago as landmarks or as records of historical events or to recall parochial missions: all these expressions and representations of simple, popular piety were profaned or destroyed. Not even the peace which we commonly accord to the dead was respected: the very symbols of our religion were uprooted from the

[1] "Evadé d'Espagne. Journal d'un prêtre." *La Croix*, October 12 to November 5, 1937.

cemeteries; graves were opened and corpses trampled underfoot.

One of the most striking phases of this persecution was the frequency of the intrusions made into private houses at all hours of the day and night, and of the minute searches carried out for any signs or traces of religious observance. In some towns savage house-by-house invasions were organized, especial attention being paid to houses previously marked down as belonging to notorious Catholics. Articles found in them were dragged or thrown into the streets and bonfires lit then and there of images, pictures, photographs, religious books and First Communion mementoes. Where the unhappy inmates begged that some of these perfectly harmless relics might be spared for their sentimental value, their requests served only to stimulate the invaders' fury and sometimes even led to the making of personal attacks upon the petitioners. From their very persons were greedily snatched such things as crosses, medals, scapulars and rosaries: occasionally resistance led to assassination, scant respect being paid either to sex or to age. Even funeral cards, kept in remembrance of departed friends or relatives, were destroyed—for did they not provide evidence of religious allegiance?

The following incident took place at San Juan de las Abadesas, a picturesque little village in the Catalan highlands, not far south of the Pyrenees, and hence very closely watched because of its nearness to the French frontier. A lady, who was visiting relatives there, was subjected to the usual vexatious personal examination. The militiawoman searching her found nothing but the funeral card of a man to whom she had been engaged. It had not occurred to her that this could possibly be confiscable. The militiawoman proceeded to tear it up, paying no heed to its owner's plea of its sentimental value. "It's no good," she said, "we have orders to destroy everything bearing the slightest connection with religion. It's much easier to pass money through than anything religious."

In order that these symbols of religious observance might be the more effectively destroyed, recourse was had to collective spoliation. In innumerable towns public criers went round the streets announcing that, under pain of alarming penalties, all books and other articles having any religious significance must be taken to the market-square to be burned. None who saw it, or the photographs taken of it, will ever forget the enormous pile of such objects which was publicly burned in the Plaza Mayor of the cathedral city of Vich.

The revolutionaries were much less interested in destroying legal instruments relating to property than in effacing evidence that individuals were practising Christians. They often had armed guards placed round banks ; but they made no attempt to defend the churches. For, over and above its being a social and political revolution, their movement was a rising against religion.

Attempts were even made to dislodge figures from the pinnacles of churches and other positions accessible only with difficulty ; sometimes the "workers" had to erect scaffolding in order to reach them. In Barcelona, for example, may be mentioned the destruction of the great crosses which surmounted the parish church of Sarriá and the Virgen Auxiliadora of the Salesians. On Tibidabo Hill, outside Barcelona, the monument to the Sacred Heart, an impressive bronze statue twenty-five feet high, was destroyed. At Manresa the revolutionaries demolished the figure of the Sacred Heart on the cupola of the convent of the Salesian nuns, formerly visible from the outskirts of the city.

Even the most venerated representations of Christ crucified were not respected. In Catalonia some of the most ancient of these have been destroyed, such as the Majestades, outstanding in the history of the world's art : the Santos Cristos de Piera at Igualada ; the Majestad of Caldas de Montbuy ; and those of Salardú and Balaguer, all objects of popular devotion. Innumerable crucifixes stolen from the churches have been used as firewood. A leading member of the French colony in Valencia was actually sent some bundles of firewood by someone on one of the revolutionary committees. Seeing that the wood was carved and of good quality, he kept it, and discovered that it consisted of a number of crucifixes, some of them of great antiquity.[1]

[1] Ives Dantun : *Valence sous la botte rouge*, Paris, 1937, pp. 161–2.

Throughout Spain the Sanctuaries of the Virgin have always been greatly venerated. They are linked with age-old traditions and outstanding events in history, and they have long been vital centres of the religious life and patriotic fervour of the people. To them have flocked the inhabitants of towns and villages, peasants, seafaring folk, persons from every class of society and from every trade and profession. Even the indifferent and the unbelieving were not wholly free from their influence.

But for the Terror, the people would never have allowed their destruction. They were the " hauts lieux où soufflait l'Espagne ". Covadonga, Nuria, La Virgen de los Desamparados, Begoña, La Merced: these and many other sanctuaries, even the humblest, speak of the things of the spirit and their profanation is a crime committed against humanity, since for generations the Spanish people have found in them comfort and inspiration.

For this reason the most valiant efforts have been made to save the images of Our Lady, the loss of which would afflict numberless Christian souls. Let us pay homage to one heroic priest who saved a historic image as the great sanctuary which had been its home went up in flames, and escaped with it over mountains and through forests, between perils of nature and perils from his own unhappy countrymen, until, at the end of a twenty-three-hour journey, he arrived, with feet torn and bleeding, at the Pyrenean frontier and gave his precious burden into safe custody. Let us also render a tribute of gratitude, due both from religion and from culture, to the efficiency and the good-will of those well-intentioned leaders who saved the thousand-year-old Sanctuary of Montserrat, the spiritual metropolis of the history and the faith of Catalonia, and for Spain as a whole an ineffaceable memorial of the devotion of her kings, immortalized in the *Cantigas* of Alfonso the Wise.

The sacrilege committed by the revolutionaries also includes the utilization of important churches for profane ends and the demolition of many others. The Cathedral of Solsona, transformed into a public market, is typical of a use to which numerous other churches have been put. An example of the conversion of churches into storehouses for victuals, munitions, vehicles, and all kinds of other things is the Cathedral of Valencia, which the revolutionaries actually opened to the passage of waggons and mules laden with merchandise. A huge list might be compiled of churches which were demolished. Santa Ana, San Francisco, San José, San Martín, Sans, Bonanova, Escolapias, Teresas, Hospitalet: all these are in Barcelona. In Gerona, Salesianos, Mercadal, Bernardas; at Olot, the Virgen del Tura; at Vich, Santa Clara, Remey and Merced; at Manresa, Santo Domingo, Carmen and San Miguel; at Mataró, the exquisite convent of the Teresas, the convents of the Benedictine and the Capuchin nuns and the Church of Providencia. The stones of the Santuario del Tura, at Olot, were used for the construction of the new market.

Everywhere the efficiency with which the destruction was carried out was rivalled only by the offensiveness and ribaldry which accompanied the work of destruction. Petrol and dynamite were part of the incendiaries' equipment; so were incendiary bombs and inflammable liquids. Little need be said of the blasphemous oaths and sacrilegious jests, or of the masquerades carried out with the sacred ornaments. Outside the churches, militiamen in episcopal mitres could be seen keeping guard or standing in confessional boxes, while others, dressed in sacerdotal vestments, would hold their orgies within.

Statues were swathed in red flags, or adorned with red ties, and made to carry weapons. At the parish church of San José in the Calle de Alcalá, Madrid, a figure of the Child Jesus was dressed up, pistol in hand, as a Communist militiaman. At the Convent of the Magdalenas, in the Calle de Hortaleza, also in Madrid, an image of the Virgin was displayed in the uniform of a militiawoman.

On many occasions the faithful were themselves compelled to take part in the work of profanation. Thus at Gerona fifty-two priests who had been seized and thrown into prison were employed on the demolition of churches, their overseer mocking them as they worked and promising a good meal as a bonus to the man who worked hardest. As recently as September 1937 some of these priests were still at work on the destruction of the church of the Salesians.

The harm done by such vandalism to culture cannot but shock the civilized world, which is no less an interested party than Spain herself. Some day the world will realize with shame that it made no attempt to intervene in this campaign of destruction waged not only against religion, but against religious art. The extent of the mischief wrought is indescribable. Great cities have lost monuments dating from the Renaissance or the Middle Ages as well as others more modern. Monasteries and mansions have disappeared, and with them their pictures, libraries and archives. Many places rich in historical memories will no longer be visited by scholars eager to learn from them of the past. It is the entire history of a people that the revolutionaries have tried to destroy: it is the life of the spirit in the widest sense of that word that has suffered persecution. Dynamite was exploded within the immense nave of Gerona Cathedral, a building unique of its kind in the whole world. With dynamite, too, an attempt was made to destroy the Arco de Bará, a magnificent Roman arch situated on the road between Barcelona and Tarragona, and nearly two thousand years old.

In the years to come, foreigners who have no idea what ravages can be wrought upon civilization by barbarism and anarchy will learn the lesson by making pilgrimages of humiliation through our country. A French review, *L'Illustration*, has already, as it were, anticipated such a pilgrimage by publishing a special issue "dedicated to the martyrdom of works of art in Spain", illustrated by a comparatively small but significant number of reproductions chosen from more than five hundred photographs taken in fourteen of the provinces liberated from Red rule. "It is simply because of their religious character", remarks *L'Illustration*, "that these great works of art have become a prey to the vandals. The degradations, mutilations and profanations, unimpeachable evidence for which can be found in them, are not attributable to acts of war. . . . Almost the whole of these works of art, which have been deliberately and systematically reduced to the state in which they now lie, are far from the battle-zones, and much of the destruction was done at times when the Government was in complete control of the regions in which they are to be found. . . . The vandals did not yield to some sudden and unpremeditated wave of passion. They obeyed orders received from committees of the local Soviets which had taken the place of the regular authorities, and these no doubt, in their turn, were carrying out instructions from higher bodies—if not from Madrid, Valencia or Barcelona, then from the Communist International."

There is no exaggeration in these words. The theft from Toledo Cathedral of that unique manuscript known as the Bible of St. Louis and the destruction of the famous Custodia, ten feet in height, wrought in the sixteenth century by Enrique de Arfe, which was smashed to pieces and left on the floor with other *débris* are typical of the destructiveness of the Reds and their eagerness to annihilate the entire spiritual heritage of our country. Many venerable and valuable art treasures, too, which had been used for worship, were taken from churches in Madrid and Barcelona and sent to the Central Museum of the Godless in Moscow, where they bear a revealing witness to the nature of the sentiments that inspired the Revolution.

Even the countryside, humanized as it had been by religion and art, would have contributed its quota to the sacrifice were it not that many towers with their belfries were found difficult to demolish and are thus still standing, solemnly testifying to the spiritual civilization of each town and village which without their churches would be but bodies without souls. The bell-towers are immovable sentries awaiting the return of a higher life, ever old and ever new, which is already on the way: dumb for a time though they be, they speak eloquently of immortality. This higher life, when fully restored, will be accompanied by the restoration of every aspect of the religious consciousness which the Revolution has attempted to eradicate. Among other things, it will restore the original names of the numerous towns, villages and streets which were so senselessly changed whenever they had any connection with religion. During the months of January and February 1937 alone, the autonomous Government of Catalonia issued seven decrees authorizing in all some ninety-six changes of this kind, most of them substituting a secular name for the name of a saint. In one of this Government's official bulletins, issued at the beginning of February 1938, was published a further list of one hundred and ten villages the names of which were changed for the same reason.

So the churches went up in flames, objects and symbols of religious significance were destroyed or profaned, bells were silent on the Lord's Day, altars were broken, the faithful were dispersed, and the use of names recalling God or the Saints was forbidden. Yet even this was not sufficient for the revolutionaries: they must needs uproot from the speech of men the name of the Almighty Himself. Everyone knows that the commonest form of greeting amongst Spaniards is the brief and eminently Christian *Adiós*,[1] a salutation which is a continual evocation of God's dominion over man and a public confession of His being our eternal Goal and the perpetual object of our adoration. This word *Adiós*, so deeply enrooted among us that it was even wont to escape the revolutionaries involuntarily, has also been subjected to the most violent persecution. Penalties have been imposed for its use; and in Aragon the Anarchist leader Ascaso ordered the substitution for it of the phrase *Sin-Dios*.[2]

Finally, let it be noted that the iconoclasts have not neglected to destroy such relics of the Saints as they could lay their hands on. Either by fire or by other means they have destroyed the bodies of San Pascual Baylón, San Bernardo Calvó, San Narciso and Beata Beatriz de Silva, together with relics of San Cugat, Beato Pedro Almató and many others.

During the pillaging and burning of the churches, historic tombs, some of them containing bodies of saints, were singled out for destruction with especial care. From the thousand-year-old monastery of Ripoll the remains of the Counts of Barcelona, founders of the Catalan royal dynasty, were taken and thrown into the river. No greater respect was accorded to Bishop Morgades, to whose piety we owe the restoration of this monastery and also the foundation

[1] [Lit.: "To God." Cf. our "Good-bye" = "God be with you."—Tr.]
[2] [I.e. "Without God"; "Godless."—Tr.]

of the Diocesan Museum of Vich, the most important institution for the preservation of historical and archæological treasures to be found in Spain. In Vich Cathedral and in the Convent of La Merced in the same city were profaned the tombs of the Catalan evangelist Blessed Antonio María Claret, of the great nineteenth-century philosopher Balmes and of the notable historian Bishop Torras y Bages. Thus in one place alone the Christian and civil traditions of our people were symbolically profaned by the enemies of civilization.

Fortunately, two famous relics have been preserved, as it were, by a miracle. The arm of the martyr Santa Tecla, Patroness of Tarragona, and the hand of Santa Teresa, which had been stolen from a monastery at Ronda, were found in the baggage of General Villalba when this was captured by the Nationalists on their entry into Málaga. Thus the relics of at least two saints—the second our Spanish saint *par excellence*—continue to bear witness to the depth and excellence of the Christian faith as it has taken root in our own country.

CHAPTER VI

PERSECUTION OF THE MINISTERS OF GOD

In no other period of persecution have such determined attempts been made to exterminate the clergy. This aim was so relentlessly and ruthlessly pursued that clergy-hunts became general. That the instructions given were quite definite many facts have proved. The President of the Revolutionary Committee of N—— stated that, together with all the committees of Catalonia, he had received the following orders: "With regard to priests, have no mercy on them and take no prisoners, but without exception kill them all." The President of the Committee of B—— consulted the Central Committee as to what was to be done with a kindly priest who was greatly respected and loved in the country. The reply was brutal: "You have had your orders: kill them all and let those you call the best and holiest be killed first."[1]

The terrible result of all this is well known, but one shudders to think of what the extent of the martyrology will be when it is completed.

In the Bishops' *Joint Letter* the number of victims is given as being ten Bishops and six thousand priests—this including the diocesan clergy alone: the final number will be still greater. Of monks, friars and nuns not less than 1600 have been killed: the figures for twenty-seven Orders and Congregations total 1379. In twenty-three of the sixty dioceses in Spain the persecution was violent and widespread. In nine of these, 80 per cent of the clergy were assassinated; in the diocese of Málaga, 50 per cent of the secular clergy and 75 per cent of the regulars. In the diocese of Toledo only five or six survive out of 110; in that of Santander, sixty out of 517.

[1] "Evadé d'Espagne. Journal d'un prêtre." *La Croix*. Feuilleton, No. 2.

The characteristics of the persecution of the clergy, then, are in a class of their own. There has been a marked interest taken in the extermination of the Church's ministers, many of whom exercised the strongest influence for good upon the social life of their communities as well as upon the faithful. Of the great number of those who are known to have perished, it is startling to find how many were eminent in the fields of literature or theology, in both general and specialized forms of culture, and in good works and institutional activities of all kinds, whether primarily religious in nature or social and popular. To cut off such persons is to deprive the community of its highest assets and to humiliate and weaken the entire sphere of civil society and hinder its progress.

Bishops, parish priests, canons, professors, directors, preachers, writers have been persecuted with particular severity. Parish priests constitute the largest proportion of the victims. The very mention of the name "Rector" (the usual name popularly applied to a parish priest in Catalonia) sufficed to set a man-hunt in operation. In one large city the house of a certain lawyer was searched and a professional certificate was found on the premises, signed by the "Rector"—i.e., Vice-Chancellor—of his University. The ignorant men, seeing the hated word, decided that he must be a priest in disguise, and the wretched lawyer, who was in fact a married man with a family, had the greatest difficulty imaginable clearing himself.

That the revolutionary committees must have ordered the extermination of all parish priests is quite evident from what happened. On arriving in a town or village, each group of incendiaries went straight for them and hunted them out with a particularly savage fury, whereas their parishioners generally tried to defend and hide them and sometimes even the local Committees would get them into safety. This explains why, in towns and villages off the beaten track, priests were trusting enough to remain for some days in their own houses, and why nearly all the older ones have perished. Not even men of over sixty were spared: and there were many of these—sixty-five of them in the diocese of Gerona alone.

A good example of this is the case of the old parish priest of the little hamlet of Alp, situated at the foot of the Pyrenees, not far from the frontier town of Puigcerdà. This good old man was defended by his parishioners, but ferreted from his hiding-place and murdered by the barbarous militiamen from Puigcerdà. The assassins, on their arrival, ordered the villagers to burn their own church and kill their *cura*. At the point of the revolver they did the first, but flatly refused to do any harm to their Rector. The militiamen threatened them with death if they disobeyed. At last the good old priest begged that they would allow him to die while his church was still burning, and in sight of the flames, but that first of all they would let him address a few words to his flock. So he gathered them together and made them a moving little homily just as he might have done from the pulpit on a festival, ending by absolving his enemies, blessing his flock and making the sign of the cross in preparation for death. But the people were more determined than ever to have nothing to do with his assassination. So the militiamen levelled their rifles to fire on them. Then their priest raised his voice for the last time.

"Fire, children," he cried, "don't be afraid. If you don't, you will only be killed too. For your sakes I die willingly."

Then a violent detonation was heard and to their horror the villagers saw him fall, shot through the head almost as his gentle voice finished speaking.[1]

Neither infirmity nor physical or mental incapacity exempted any priest from the persecution. There are numerous cases of priests who were seriously ill and who were dragged by force from hospitals or from their homes. Such were Father Miralpeix, a priest from Castelló d'Ampurias, Father Condamines, of Tárrega, and a third priest who who lived in the Colonia Bonmatí, near Gerona. The priest of a Figueras church, Father Casademont, an old man, almost blind, was critically ill when his assassins carried him away and killed him. Another priest in the same city, Father Murtra, had just undergone an operation. Suffering from acute neurasthenia, he was taken to a sanatorium at Salt, and, in filling up the necessary admission form for

[1] [Confirmation of all the details in this story has not been possible.—Tr.]

him, his friends concealed the fact that he was in Holy Orders. One day, when his pain was so severe that it lessened his self-control he happened to let fall the words: "When I was a priest. . . ." Some militiamen, hearing of this, came and murdered him. Equally barbarous was the murder of the Archpriest of Oropesa. This old man of seventy was dying and had already received the last Sacraments. None the less, a gang of militiamen dragged him from his bed and shot him.[1]

The priest-hunts took the most desperate and inhuman forms. On several occasions they were stimulated by means of money prizes. At Vich, where the fun was raging fast and furious as late as May 1937, a prize of two hundred pesetas[2] was offered for every betrayal of a priest's hiding-place. In a Barcelona newspaper a very large sum, fifteen thousand pesetas, was offered for the capture of a certain Jesuit. The priest, no doubt, was safer if he fled to the mountains than if he remained in a human habitation, but even here his safety was not assured. Hounds were requisitioned for some of the priest-hunts, so that the fugitives could be pursued over hill and dale; the narratives of the survivors make one shudder. The Mayor of Falset, a small town in the province of Tarragona, issued a public proclamation, inviting all who had dogs and guns to help hunt the *curas*, whom he himself had been instrumental in driving to the mountains. After weeks and weeks of a life more easily imagined than described, priests have been found in the most lamentable states—some starving, some dying of inanition. Occasionally, rather than perish of hunger, they gave themselves up and took their chance at the hands of the Revolutionary Committees, having discovered to their cost how the country-folk and mountain-dwellers were paralysed out of their usually abundant kindness by sheer terror. In the corner of the vault of a parish church in Barcelona which had been destroyed were found the dead

[1] These details are taken from the accounts of what happened in parishes near Oropesa, in the dioceses of Toledo and Ávila, which have been collected by P. Teodoro Toni, S.J., and excerpted by P. Constantino Bayle in his pamphlet *¿ Qué pasa en España ? A los católicos del mundo.* Salamanca, 1937, pp. 61–62.

[2] [£8 at par.—Tr.]

bodies of three priests. Someone who had had the courage to bring food to them in their hiding-place night by night had been captured, and when they found that his visits had ceased, they preferred starving to coming out and facing destruction.

There have been repeated cases of shootings of priests and religious *en masse*. The Dominican Fathers of Madrid were treated barbarously. From a cellar in the Cuesta de Santo Domingo in the same city were dragged eighteen nuns, Adoratrices, and brutally assassinated. In the Casa de Campo, sixty-eight priests were killed on one occasion alone. Similar accounts could be given of the Augustinians of El Escorial, the Mercedarians of Portell, the Franciscans of Berga, the Claretians of Cervera and Barbastro, the Carmelites of Tárrega, the Benedictines of El Pueyo, the Bishop of Barbastro with a large number of his priests, the group of clergy and laity who went to their deaths with the Bishop of Lérida, the three hundred who were deported from Jaén with their Bishop, and who met their fate on the Puente de Vallecas.

At Sigüenza, a group of forty, half of whom were priests and half students from a seminary, were taken from prison on to the highroad so that their captors might have the sport of shooting them as they tried to escape: instead of doing this, they all knelt down and were shot as they prayed. At Toledo, on several occasions, condemned priests were taken in batches to the place of their execution, reciting the Rosary as they went. On August 7, 1936, a correspondent of the *Morning Post*, recently come from Valencia, gave a terrible account of the atrocities which he had seen in that city, where, for example, forty-six priests, who had gathered into one room, were hideously murdered. The Dominicans, both Fathers and students, from the Novice-House and Seminary of Calanda and Ocaña, suffered badly. Nor was the most elementary respect shown for the peace and welfare of orphanages and hospices. Seven brothers of the Order of St. John of God were dragged from a Málaga sanatorium and killed, while twenty-two lost their lives in the fine sanatorium of Calafell, an establishment erected for the treatment of scrofulous children, so well known throughout

Catalonia that public collections for it at railway-stations and other places used to be authorized. These Calafell brothers were taken in lorries through the town of Vedrell before being executed. Some of them stood erect ; others knelt in prayer ; and others spent the time singing hymns or shouting *vivas* to Christ the King.

In La Torrasa, the suburb of Barcelona most infested by the ruthless immigrants from Murcia who have been such a strength to the Anarchists, some of the gangs discovered that a number of priests had taken refuge in the environs of Torelló ; at the beginning of October 1936, therefore, they organized a raid in which eighteen of these priests perished. At Moncada five Brothers of Christian Doctrine were killed and with them four priests and forty of the laity.

If it was possible to dishonour the victims, the murderers never failed to do this. Here are two typical cases.

One is the exhumation of the bodies of Salesian nuns in Barcelona. Nineteen such corpses were exhibited outside the broad and handsome façade of the Salesian Church, and made the butt of obscene jests by self-appointed showmen. This is a somewhat macabre instance of the anti-clerical hatred, the aim of which was to excite the masses to violence and persecution. And those responsible appear not to have been ashamed of themselves : M. Bloch, indeed, still makes ironical comments upon the bodies of those nuns.

The second example is the mass assassination of a large number of Marist Brothers. The passport offices controlled by two members of the Anarchist High Command had agreed, upon receipt of a large sum of money, to allow some two hundred Marists to embark with a great many other fugitives. But shortly before the boat left they were all forced to disembark again : ninety-two of them were executed ; the remainder, imprisoned. The charge brought against them was that their luggage was full of plans, maps and other papers which incriminated them in accusations of espionage on behalf of the enemy. Pillage, extermination, dishonour : what a fate for those unfortunate Brothers !

The extermination of religious and priests was carried out without mercy. The parish priest of Tordera was seriously wounded outside the village; as with tremulous hands he groped his way along a wall he left marks of blood which led to the discovery of his hiding-place to which he was traced and there murdered.

Numerous cases have been reported in which safe-conducts for use within Spain or passports for abroad were given, containing secret marks which indicated that the bearers were to be killed; the wretched bearers, thinking themselves safe, presented their papers and found themselves seized and condemned to be shot.

Even official safe-conducts and diplomatic passports sometimes proved to be death-warrants.

Early in 1938 the Government of Madrid paid the Government of Colombia an indemnification of 250,000 pesos for the families of "nine Colombian subjects who had met their deaths during the Spanish War". Tragic euphemism! The Consul-General of Colombia, trusting the formal guarantees given him by the Madrid Government, had sent seven of his compatriots, religious of the Order of St John of God, to Barcelona, accompanied by a chauffeur; at Barcelona they were to embark for their own country. All of them carried passports in order, and all wore armlets of the Colombian colours bearing the seal of the Colombian Legation. On their arrival at Barcelona, on August 8, 1936, they were assassinated, and the militias to which the authors of so monstrous a crime belonged reported the fact to the Colombian Consul-General at Barcelona. At Zafra, in the province of Badajoz, a Colombian theological student, belonging to the Community of the Sacred Heart of Mary, was also foully assassinated, despite his having been provided with a safe-conduct delivered by the Governor of Ciudad Real.[1]

Numerous and varied are the cases in which victims have been lured to their deaths by pretences of confidence or false protection. Here is a cruel and cynical example. At Sabadell, one of the most populous towns in Catalonia, the apologist, Sardá y Salvany, a great man who enjoyed universal prestige, had given up his magnificent mansion and converted it into a Hospice for the Aged Poor, making

[1] Memorandum by the Colombian Minister of Foreign Affairs, presented to Parliament, pp. 166–74. Cf. *Bulletin d'Information Espagnole*, No. 516.

over to the foundation the whole of his wealth and taking for himself only the duties of their chaplain. It would have been difficult to find an act of greater abnegation or one which had made its author more widely beloved. Upon the founder's death, his place was taken by another priest, Father Cayetano Clausellas, whom the poorest and humblest called the " Saint ", for no priest had ever been known to be so diligent in visiting the poor. When the Revolution broke out, he was seventy-five years of age ; and he stayed in the Hospice, in which there were about a hundred inmates, not counting the nuns who attended them, for nobody thought that such an institution could possibly be attacked. But a few days later, revolutionaries came to look for the " Saint ", and, under the pretext of taking him to a place of greater safety, they led him away and shot him. It was a shameful act, which roused the whole city, for Father Clausellas was a man whom the people had, as it were, canonized during his lifetime.

If further examples are needed, there is the fate of Father José Rubiol, aged sixty-four, who was left half dead for forty-eight hours in a field. A militiaman, passing, heard his groans. The priest begged him for a glass of water. Instead of giving it to him, he took a handful of fire-wood, set light to it and held it to his clothes till they caught fire.

The Sanatorium of Fontilles, in the province of Valencia, was a Jesuit foundation doing splendid work for lepers. When the Society of Jesus in Spain was dissolved in 1932, Father Bori, the Director of the Sanatorium, went to live in the Convent of the Little Sisters of the Poor in Valencia. Here this most popular benefactor of the lepers was sought out and killed.[1]

The story of the martyrdom of the Jesuit Fathers Cots and Romá and of Brother Iriondo, as told by the former Provincial, Father José M. Murall, has received wide publicity.[2] Father Murall was shot with them and fell seriously wounded, but was able to make a dramatic escape. This is a most vivid testimony of how good men die for the Faith and also

[1] A.B.C.D. : *Cento Martiri della Rivoluzione del* 1936 *nella Catalogna*, Genoa, 1937.

[2] [Cf. *La Persécution religieuse en Espagne*, Paris, 1937, pp. 168–72. —Tr.]

of the nature of the numerous assassinations which took place at La Rabassada, near Barcelona.

The chaplain of the Franciscan nuns at Oropesa, in the province of Toledo, was brutally mutilated and then made to act as the victim in a kind of human bullfight in the market-place. The same sport was practised with the parish priest at Alcañizo. A friar at Rielves, in the same province, and several laymen, had their eyes put out and were then beaten and thrown, while still alive, into a well. The Archpriest of Talavera was also made sport with in a mock bullfight, held in the courtyard of a seminary of which he had been the leading spirit. They stuck knives into him for *banderillas* and finally shot him.

Here is an example of how anti-religious frenzy dominated all other passions in these revolutionaries. Passing through Lérida on its way to the Aragonese front, the famous Durruti column observed that the Cathedral had not been harmed. Thereupon, mocking their Lérida comrades for their cowardly dereliction of duty, they remedied the matter by setting fire to it themselves—and so thoroughly that the fire lasted for two whole days. Another detachment of militia on its way to the front heard that the Bishop of Barbastro was imprisoned, with many priests and religious, in his cathedral city. So before going farther they did what the militia in Barbastro itself had not dared to do.

At Matadapera, near Tarrasa, the parish priest happened to be in his church when the incendiaries seized its contents in order to burn them. Seeing that they were about to lay hold on a statue of Christ, he approached them hurriedly. "Let me go to the fire instead of the Christ!" he begged. The only answer of the militiamen was to fell him to the ground with a heavy blow.

But what was denied to this good priest was granted to others.

In the market-place of Cervera a huge bonfire was made of statues and articles of worship. The organist of the church, Father Obiols, who had been tortured till hardly any life was left in him, was carried to the fire and thrown upon it. In a village in the east of Spain the parish priest was thrown on a similar fire and burned alive.

What a holocaust—the living servant of God sacrificed together with the lifeless matter which has been fashioned for His honour and service! Only one other holocaust has surpassed it—that of the priest who gave his life while saying Mass in the chapel of the Sanatorium at Tarrasa. His presence there was discovered by the chance fact that the server was heard ringing the altar-bell. He was shot while actually celebrating the Holy Sacrifice at the altar.

CHAPTER VII

HATRED OF GOD AND ANTI-RELIGIOUS SADISM

ONE of the most striking features of the Spanish persecution is the frenzy manifested not only toward the victims of the persecution but toward God and the Saints. In all revolutions the bestial element in man is to a greater or a lesser extent unleashed—a fact which accounts for the cases which always occur in them of blasphemous mockery and horseplay, the mutilation of statues and the profanation of cemeteries. It may be doubted, however, if in any persecution there has been such a gigantic and diabolical manifestation of rancour, directed of set purpose against God, as in the Spanish Revolution. One day, soon after it began, a Red orator said over the wireless : " They say on the other side that God is on the side of Franco. I don't know if that is true, but I do know that Satan is on our side." A stupid remark, intended presumably to be taken as a jest—but events have proved that it was only too true.

Let us quote a few examples.

Some of the gangs of incendiaries, in their tours of certain districts, have frequently and systematically begun their desecrations of churches by levelling their rifles at the Tabernacle.

A horrible feature of these attacks on churches has been the profanation of the Sacred Host, and too often there has been no time to effect its salvation. In some of the churches of the diocese of Ávila (in the province of Toledo), the Host was trampled underfoot. At Vich Cathedral, where the attack was made by the most desperate gangs of La Torrasa, the invaders rushed to the Tabernacle, shouting insults against the Pope and against religion. When they found it empty, their fury knew no bounds. " Where have they put that stuff they call God ? " they shouted.

The life-like figure of Our Lord known as the Santo Cristo de Balaguer, impressive both by its size and by the sublimity of its expression, might be expected to have excited the admiration even of those who came to profane it. On the contrary, it was hacked with amazing zest into the smallest pieces: this surely suggests a very different spirit from that which was content with throwing such figures in motley heaps on to the flames.

At Toledo, in the summer of 1936, the militiamen seized the famous Cristo de la Vega and carried it to the Plaza de Zocodover, which faces the great Alcázar, well known for the siege which it was then undergoing. Under the eyes of the brave garrison they brandished the figure aloft and cried: "Here we have the Cristo de la Vega! We're going to burn it. If you are Catholics, come down and stop us. We'd stop you all right if you did the same with a figure of Lenin. Now let's see if you come down!"

A few moments passed. From the Alcázar could be heard the blows of the axes destroying the figure of the Crucified. Soon what remained of the Cristo de la Vega was feeding the flames. But two of the gang, in their eagerness to stoke them, imprudently got into the line of fire, and a well-aimed volley from the watchful Alcázar garrison not only shot them dead, but pitched them on to the bonfire.[1]

Some of the incidents in which profanations of this kind took place seem to have been suggested by Soviet plays and films, in which the trial of Jesus Christ is parodied in terms of the modern persecutions organized by the Godless.

In a village near Valencia, for example, an image of the Archangel St. Michael was solemnly tried by the Revolutionary Committee, condemned to death and given a public execution. In the Alfambra zone, where statues have been found of which the faces have been riddled with bullets, a figure of the Virgin of Carmel was publicly shot, and children coming out from school were invited to be present. Can anyone imagine a more repugnant sight than the conversion of the Sign of our salvation into an instrument of murder? An Italian legionary, in the course of some moving letters,

[1] From the paper *Extremadura* (October 15, 1936), cit. J. Arrarás and L. Jordana, *El Sitio del Alcázar*, Saragossa, 1937, p. 196.

tells of having seen dead bodies of which the heads had been mutilated by blows with an iron crucifix.

And must we not give the fullest symbolic value to the ecstasy of anti-religious frenzy which led to the shooting of the statue erected some years ago to the Sacred Heart on the Hill of the Angels—or the Hill of the Reds, as it was renamed after that event. Not only is this of significance because of what that statue meant as a symbol of Spain's re-dedication to Christ but also because the revolutionaries themselves had photographs taken of their attempt to destroy it and caused these to be given the widest circulation.

The whole of the cultured world feels deeply about the destruction of works of religious art on account of their artistic value and is aware that masterpieces of painting and sculpture have been lost for ever. Let it be remembered that the profanation of the idea signified is more terrible even than that of the outward sign. It constitutes an attack upon the divine and supernatural world, which goes deeper than a mere attempt to destroy articles used in public worship and to impede a Christian in the profession of his faith.

It suffices to look at those figures of Christ and the Virgin with their eyes brutally put out, at the canvases and reredoses ripped by bayonets, and at the statues smashed into the smallest pieces, to gain some idea of the force of this explosion of hatred of God. To destroy such things was not enough. The vandals looked gloatingly at these representations of Divinity and sanctity as though they were living beings for whom they cherished a deadly hatred and would fain have subjected to torture with a passion that was subhuman and a fury manifested alike in their gestures and their blasphemous cries.

In all the provinces that have been freed from Red rule undeniable documentary evidence of this passion can be given. The reredoses of churches provided excellent targets. Statues have been found smashed to pieces by hammers, mutilated by being stoned, decapitated or otherwise barbarously injured. Admirable examples of Castilian or Andalusian carving, often in polychrome, have been destroyed by axes ; heads and legs have been hacked off and faces split from top to bottom ; others have been chopped into fragments and then burned. Valuable statues of alabaster and marble have been smashed to pieces. Most remarkable is the extraordinary frequency of that particular sadistic urge which finds satisfaction in putting out the eyes of these figures, the action being sometimes accompanied by refinements of cruelty. Some of the finest work in gold and silver has been destroyed and the pieces have been heaped up on church floors: included in this category are tabernacles, custodia and reliquaries of the greatest value. Such things have even been found in Red trenches captured by the Nationalists. Sometimes the degradation of the vandals has been such that they have gone so far as to sign their handiwork: on the breast of a mutilated figure of Christ, or of a Saint, on torn canvases and mutilated reredoses of great beauty have been found the letters F.A.I. or C.N.T.[1]

Among the forms of torture employed by the revolutionaries are some clearly inspired by the histories of the Saints. There is, for example, the singular case of Dr. Francisco Bover, *ecónomo* of the parish of Sidamunt, in the province of Lérida. This victim of the persecution was flayed alive, like St Bartholomew, after which his body, torn and bleeding as it was, served as a target for his torturers' rifles.

One dramatic narrative, published by the Entente Internationale Anti-Communiste, centres around a Czecho-Slovakian missionary, a priest of the Orthodox Church, who was imprisoned for several months in Málaga until he was saved by British intervention. This priest was condemned to death because a photograph had been found on him which represented him saying Mass in Africa. The sentence was passed by a Jewish tailor hailing from Odessa who was in the habit of adorning his speeches with pseudo-theological sarcasm. One day he announced that he was about to send fifteen of his prisoners by express train to Heaven as he understood that the Almighty God had urgent need of their souls to intercede with Him on behalf of Franco. When he observed the terror of the remaining prisoners he declared

[1] Cf. the photographs reproduced in the issue of *L'Illustration* already referred to.

that he would send St. Peter another soul, this time to intercede with God for the liberation of the remainder from their Communist prison, and that, as St. Peter only understood Latin, the new victim would have to be a priest. One of his frequent sallies was the remark that he had forgotten to dispatch any souls to Heaven that day and that he would have to pay God the necessary interest by sending a few more than usual: this would account for the dispatch of a dozen or so more victims.[1]

A particularly odious mark of revolutionary sadism and hatred of God has been the reproduction of details of the Passion of Our Lord.

Among the victims of the persecution to be crucified were a number of persons at Fuenterrabía, a seminarist at Barbastro, the parish priest of Torrijos, a hermit at Játiva and several lay persons at Almendralejo, in the province of Badajoz, who were crucified first and afterwards burned alive.

At Fuenterrabía, on a hot summer's day, a number of monks were laid on their backs on the roof of a monastery and secured, first with cords, and afterwards with nails, with their arms extended and their faces unprotected from the blazing sun. After a few hours of this torture they were pelted with grenades and dynamite and so destroyed.

In one of the squares of the city of Lérida a tribunal was set up and a parody rehearsed of the trial of Christ before Pilate. The youth accused was cruelly scourged and pummelled by his captors' fists. Then he was made to stand on a table and asked who he was. "I am a Barbastro seminarist," he replied. The mob clamoured for his death. After this the commissary of the F.A.I. washed his hands, following the example of Pilate, and sentenced him to die on the cross. Stripped of his clothes and nailed to a wooden beam, he yielded up his soul to God, with the words: "Jesus, for Thy love and for the salvation of Spain."

Near Játiva there is (or was) a hill surmounted by a Calvary, with stations of the Cross erected at intervals up the slope. An old hermit, aged seventy years, who lived near the Calvary, was seized by a hundred or so rough men

[1] *Bulletin d'Information Espagnole*, No. 336.

and women, stripped naked and forced to descend the hill with them, to the accompaniment of blows with thorny switches and branches from trees. At each station they made him kneel down while they shouted insults and blasphemies at him. At the head of the procession marched a militiaman bearing a large ciborium ; this two boys dressed in surplices kept filled with wine and the victim was made to swallow copious draughts from it. At the tail of the procession was a donkey covered with a cloak embroidered with gold lace and led by another militiaman who rang an altar bell as they went along.

By the time they reached the city the old hermit was bleeding from his wounds and so exhausted that he could hardly drag himself another step. In a courtyard near the Consistory courthouse there was a large fountain. Taking him by the head and the feet, they held him under the water until he was drowned.

The martyrdom of Father Liberio González, a man of forty-two, formerly *cura* of Torrijos, who at the time of his death was parish priest of Navalmorales, took place as follows :

"I want to suffer for Christ," he said to the militiamen who had taken him prisoner.

"Oh, do you ?" they answered. "Then you shall die as Christ did."

So they stripped him and scourged him mercilessly.

"Now let's reproduce the Passion !" said one. "We'll play at Holy Week !" said another. "Yes, that will be good sport !" cried the rest.

Fastening a great beam of wood on their victim's back, they began to make game of him. They gave him vinegar to drink. They led him half-naked through the streets of Torrijos. They dressed him up as a militiaman and crowned him with thorns.

"Blaspheme and we will forgive you !" they cried at last. "It is I who forgive and bless you," replied the martyr. Then they discussed how they should finish him off. Some wanted to nail him to a cross, others to shoot him. In the end they fired volleys at him. Before his death he made one last request :

"Shoot me as I stand facing you so that I can bless you and forgive you again."

These were the last words he uttered. His tortures lasted for three days. This is surely one of the most extraordinary narratives of the persecution.[1]

We must also consider the eagerness of the persecutors to make their victims apostatize as another of the signs of their hatred of God. Their usual method of attempting to procure apostasies was the redoubling of their tortures. This was one of the most general characteristics of the persecution in Red territory. Let us cite various cases: Father Pagés, of the parish of the Conception, in Barcelona; a Benedictine monk, Father Rodamilans, at Sabadell; seven Franciscan friars, at Azuaga in the province of Badajoz; Father Miralpeix at Castelló de Ampurias. The Franciscans had their tongues cut out and their ears severed. Father Miralpeix, an invalid, they compelled to come with them half-dressed; after forbidding him to put on his cassock (because "we don't have priests any more"), they ordered him to declare that all he had ever taught was false. His only reply was: "Hail, Christ the King!"

The parish priest of San Quintín de Mediona, Father José Bellera, and his curate, were protected by the people for over a week. A gang of revolutionaries, complete strangers to the district, then came in search of them. They told the curate that he could go and his Rector advised him to accept the offer; but he preferred to stand by him. They then offered them both their lives if they would blaspheme the sacred Name of God. They refused resolutely to do so and were shot dead.

A number of Claretian novices from Cervera, whose residence was in the buildings formerly occupied by the University of that town, were also ordered to abjure their faith. Refusing to comply, they were subjected to torture. Rosary beads were thrust into their ears till the tympanum was perforated and attempts were made to force them to swallow medals and rosaries. Finally, they put them to death. The porters of the Madre de Dios Convent at Baena, in the

[1] *Bulletin d'Information Espagnole*, No. 380.

province of Córdoba, had the medals which they wore round their necks thrust into their eyes.

Some forty seminarists from Tarragona were captured at Urgel, where they were spending their vacation, and sent to Lérida prison. One of them was taken aside and told that a means should be found to save them all if he alone would deny his faith. He, too, refused; but in this case his courage and sincerity produced the opposite effect upon his persecutors; the entire group were set free and sent back in lorries to their homes.

The president of a branch of the Federation of Young Christians of Catalonia was burned alive. When his feet were half burned off they ordered him to deny his religion. With quietness and dignity he set aside the temptation and they then left him to his death.

The old parish priest of Escalona, a village in the diocese of Toledo, was told that his life would be saved if he would blaspheme and deny God in the presence of his flock. The good priest's only reply was to give a *viva* for Christ the King. The infuriated revolutionaries then dragged him to a place near the cemetery, where they shot him in the legs, again and again, till he died.

Other cases abound; that of a Jesuit at Azuaga, a spiritual director at Badajoz, the Franciscans at Fuenteovejuna, the Capuchins at Antequera, a Carmelite and a Salesian at Seville. In each of these cases hatred of religion led the persecutors to endeavour to drag blasphemies from their victims. In each they received only the martyr's cry of "Hail, Christ the King!" And the heavens opened, as with the Trisagion of the Blessed mingled the new praises of these purple-clad novices of eternity. One thinks of those words of Prudentius: *Christum negaret, quisque mallet vivere.*

In the Benedictine priory of El Pueyo, in the province of Barbastro, there were eleven monks, eleven novices and six lay brothers. All these were invited to deny their faith and thus save their lives. Before they were shot the Prior begged permission to recite the prayers for the dying. This was granted; as he prayed, his fellow-victims all joined in the responses, and finally he gave them the absolution *in articulo mortis.*

The last example to be quoted under this head is the terrible torture undergone by the *cura* of Fuenterrabía, who was imprisoned in the fortress of Guadalupe with many leaders of political life and of thought, all of whom were assassinated before the fall of Irún. The *cura* was subjected to the most sacrilegious insults and to all kinds of brutality which he bore with a superhuman patience and humility. But when they ordered him to deny the existence of God he replied with the last breath that remained to him: "Never will you persuade me to deny God, for I have dedicated my whole life to Him and He will judge you and yours."[1]

Other profanations of the most refined sort can be cited to show how the mark of the Beast stamps the leaders of the Spanish persecution.

For Carnival, in the Cathedral of Seo de Urgel, all preparations were made for the celebration of Mass at the High Altar, after which a dance was held, with the orchestra playing in the choir.

In the so-called "Church of the Sacristy", in the mediæval capital of the Cerdagne, there was a greatly venerated image known as the Virgin of Flix. The revolutionaries stripped it of its costly vestments and put these on a girl who was shameless enough to walk through the town in them, bearing the image before her. After this the image, its church and the parish church of the town were all set on fire and the two churches were later completely demolished.

The brothers Tharaud have described their visit to the celebrated Sanctuary of Montserrat, which was confiscated by the Catalan Government and thus came to no harm. A caretaker took them round, smoking a cigarette, and when they came to the celebrated figure of Our Lady—the "Black Virgin" as it is called—he amused himself by blowing the smoke into its face. A still more shocking incident took place at La Pobla de Lillet. A number of prisoners were incarcerated in a large hall, at the end of which had been placed a statue of Christ taken from the parish church. From time to time militiamen placed their lighted cigarettes in the mouth of the statue and mocked Christ and the Christian faith in order to exasperate their prisoners.

[1] [Confirmation of all the details in this story has not been possible.—Tr.]

In the church of San Miguel at Toledo, the High Altar, after being stripped, was adorned with skulls, remains unearthed from tombs and broken and mutilated images—a horrible exhibition of sacrilege and sadism.

It would be about the month of June 1937 that the valuable Custodia of Vich Cathedral, together with other articles of value which had been stolen from the Cathedral, was found in a grave in the city cemetery. The militiamen, after committing the robbery, had held a "funeral" and buried their booty with mock ceremonial.

A still more cynical ceremony occurred at the time of the murder of a priest in the village of Ametlla de Merola. Before being killed, he was led through the village of Aviá in a long procession, and as it went along burlesques of funeral dirges were sung, as though the procession were part of a Catholic funeral.

At Arenas de San Pedro, in the province of Ávila, a number of victims were imprisoned and afterwards shot. On the night before their execution the Reds dressed up in chasubles and other sacerdotal vestments, and, amid threats and blasphemies, went through a pretence of hearing their confessions. After this they organized a grotesque procession through the village, chanting responses as they went.

The outrageous perversity of these acts of incredible savagery is explicable only by Satanic delight in the perpetration of crime for its own sake. It exemplifies a new kind of sadism the intensity and extent of which had never previously been known. The very executioners gave publicity to their infamous deeds; many of these horrors of the Revolution would not even now have become known if the revolutionaries had not themselves noised them abroad. In some places they were anxious to enable the proletariat to regale themselves upon the agonies of their victims. In Madrid, with this end in view, a motor-bus service was established, running from the Plaza de España to the Pradera de San Isidro, which had become one of the principal slaughter-grounds of the Revolution.

Could any pleasure be more horrible than that of the militiaman who murdered a priest by placing him between his knees and striking him repeatedly with the butt-end of his pistol till his own clothes and his very hands were stained with his victim's blood ?

Another repulsive act was the assembling of people to witness tortures and murders. Eight priests were publicly executed in the principal square of Tremp ; and at Valls twenty persons were forced to watch their parish priest being burned alive before themselves being shot. Only mass intoxication can explain such a phenomenon of crime-psychosis as this last. But can even that account for the incident which follows ?

In Barcelona a priest was hunted down by a militiaman, who kept him for six days in his own house and treated him as an honoured guest. On the last day the two were walking together down the Ramblas, when they met some of the militiaman's friends who were just setting off for an excursion into the suburbs. Suddenly the militiaman said to his guest : " I've had enough of feeding you. Get ready for death " ; and fired his pistol at him. Then he turned to his friends, and said calmly : " He was a priest. It's a long time since I killed anybody. I just had to do it ! "

In the Karl Marx Barracks at Barcelona a prisoner overheard the following report : " Things are going on quite well. They telephoned that a priest had escaped. But we got there in time. We found him in the Vía Layetana, and *there he remained*."

Two further incidents may be added which indicate the degree of hatred and perversion which the propaganda of the Godless had instilled into their adepts, multiplying many times the fury responsible for their crimes.

When the Nationalist troops entered a certain Andalusian town they found a Red soldier wounded in the breast by a shell-splinter. Feeling that he was near his end, he asked for a priest. Subsequently he stated that with his own hand he had killed no less than thirty-two priests.

Father Juan Buixó, a sixty-year-old missionary of the Corazón de María, had previously worked as a doctor at Moncada. When the inmates of the University buildings of Cervera were forcibly dispersed, he took refuge in the Hospital, where he was able to practise his former profession. He was a man of exemplary life, deeply versed in culture.

About the middle of September a wounded youth of about twenty, from the Huesca front, was brought to the Hospital. When he was out of danger, he said to the doctor: "I know you; you were one of those fellows in the old University. I've killed sixty-seven already. You'll be the sixty-eighth. Father Buixó continued to attend him and a week later pronounced him fit to be discharged. Before leaving, the wretched youth fulfilled his promise by shooting his benefactor and improved upon it by also killing an old monk of seventy.

Let the following incident serve as a final illuminating illustration of the origins and nature of these brutal acts, and of their efficacy, as well as of the anti-religious spirit which inspired them.

When the lorries of incendiaries from La Torrasa reached the gateway of the Episcopal Palace of Vich, the militiamen, as they got down, said to someone who happened to be standing there:

"We have orders to kill all Bishops, priests and monks we find." And they set about searching the Palace.

As they were engaged in their barbarous task of destroying the statues in the Cathedral, one of them was heard to explain:

"We're following our plan; we know exactly what we have to do. I spent eighteen months in Russia and so did lots of us, and they showed us how to do it there. We've learnt to hate Christ and to wage war on Him to the death. We won't leave a single cross standing."

CHAPTER VIII

PERSECUTION OF RELIGIOUS BELIEF AND PRACTICE

ANOTHER of the outstanding characteristics of the Spanish persecution has been the attacks upon the laity for their profession and practice of the Faith. Even to be suspected of being a practising Catholic was sufficient motive for persecution ; to confess to that crime was tantamount to a conviction. The faithful laity have been persecuted no less than the clergy. The totalitarian character of the persecution has been perfectly obvious : no God, no priesthood, no church, no *plebs Christi*. The activities of the Terror which aimed at uprooting individual belief, or at driving it down into the depths of the individual conscience, were as widespread and as cruel as those directed against the churches and the ministers of the Lord. And the persecution of the laity has naturally been the more fruitful in victims.

The Pope, in his Encyclical on Communism, recognized this, and proclaimed it to the whole world :

> " In places where the scourge of Communism has not had time to make the effects of its theories felt, as in our beloved Spain, it has unleashed itself with even greater violence. It is not a question of the destruction of a church or a religious house here or there ; wherever possible, all the churches and religious houses, and everything bearing the sign of the Christian religion, have been destroyed, not excepting the most valuable monuments of art or science. Communist frenzy has not been content with assassinating Bishops, and thousands of priests, monks and nuns, nor even with making its principal victims those engaged the most zealously in charity on behalf of the workers and the poor. The

largest number of its victims come from the varied ranks of the laity, where people are still being assassinated in the mass almost daily, simply for being good Christians, or, at most, for being opposed to Communistic atheism. And this frightful destruction is being carried out with a hatred, a barbarism and a savagery which nowadays one would hardly believe possible."

It will be understood, therefore, why we devote particular attention to this aspect of the Spanish persecution.

The first and most general form taken by the persecution of the faithful laity was the spoliation of Christian homes of all articles and symbols connected with religion. The victims of this phase of the persecution, who were very numerous, were punished by the loss or destruction of all their property, by prolonged imprisonment, by torture, even by death. No respect was paid to womanly modesty by those who saw the chance of snatching the medals, crosses, or scapulars which Spanish women always wear, and which hitherto have invariably been respected. Such a practice is a private and individual act of homage to God, the Virgin and the Saints, and a personal expression and an inviolable reminder of what has to do only with God and the individual soul. One day we may know how many people have lost their lives during the persecution for having in their possession rosaries, which in Spain are so favourite an accompaniment of prayer and are as invariably to be found in the houses of the faithful and as carefully preserved as their identity-cards.

A monk who was escaping from Cervera found the body of a young man whose face was completely disfigured by knife-wounds. Believing that he recognized him, he searched in his pocket and found a rosary. "Here," he said to himself, "must be the reason for his death and his title-deeds to the honour of martyrdom."

A typical case of this kind is that of the oldest member of the French colony of Bilbao, who was assassinated at Santander because a militiaman saw him hiding his rosaries in a heap of straw while an examination of his belongings was proceeding.

Before going farther, however, let us hasten to say that in order to prove that the faithful were persecuted in this way, following a carefully organized plan and obeying strict instructions, there is no need to have recourse to injunctions given to our Communist youth such as that published in *La Vanguardia* for November 20, 1936, which announces that "Men may be arrested and shot solely for being Catholics." There is juridical evidence for these facts, which is more revealing than the facts themselves; it furnishes an illuminating proof of the important part played by the persecution of beliefs in the general extermination of the various social classes. Such evidence can be found in the publicity given by the Red Press itself to police activities and to the sentences passed by the Popular Tribunals. We shall cite a few cases taken at random, principally from the Barcelona Press, and dated months after the outbreak of the Revolution.

The Fourth Popular Tribunal had before it two brothers, Guillermo and José Pérez Rodrigo, who were accused of having been employed as workmen in the former Salesian Convent. Only one witness appeared against them, who affirmed that Guillermo had worn an ecclesiastical habit. The other witnesses were favourable to the accused. The fiscal asked that Guillermo should be executed and his brother given five years' imprisonment.[1]

A priest, Pedro Lisbona Alonso, was tried by the Third Popular Tribunal, and here, too, the fiscal asked for a death sentence. The accused had been a leading member of the staff of the Barcelona newspaper *El Correo Catalán*, "a paper which made propaganda against the Left."[2] The prestige which he enjoyed as a journalist and his own eloquent defence secured a reduction of the sentence to thirty years' imprisonment.

Father Francisco Beicochea Aguirre, a Discalced Carmelite friar seventy-eight years of age, had come from Chile four months before the outbreak of the Revolution to take part in a Eucharistic Congress. He was brought before the First Popular Tribunal on the charge of having taken part

[1] *La Vanguardia*, December 8, 1936.
[2] *Ibid.*, December 26, 1936.

in the insurrection. Here, too, the fiscal asked for a death sentence.[1]

For the same reason the Principal of the College of Marist Brothers at Vich was condemned to death.[2]

In a house in the Ronda de Fermín Salvochea, the police arrested two men and four women whom they had surprised at Mass. They had unfortunately been unable to effect the arrest of the celebrant.[3]

The agents of the anti-Fascist brigade learned that meetings were being held in a house in the Calle de Tabern, situated in the Barcelona suburb of San Gervasio ; after watching the house, they succeeded in arresting the culprits in their own homes. One of them, a youth living in the Calle de Cortes, was convicted because an oratory and various articles used for Divine worship were found in his house. The total number of those arrested was ten ; all of them had indulged in religious practices. In the house of the religious who used to say Mass for them, a certain Father Nolla, of the Corazón de María, were found moulds for the making of wafer bread, and a sum of money. From the latter discovery it was deduced that this priest had been collecting funds and devoting them to the religious practices in which he indulged together with the rest of the accused.[4]

The vigilance of the agents of the same brigade led to the discovery, in a house in the Avenida del Catorce de Abril, of a meeting of five persons who were about to take part in a religious marriage ceremony. The priest was found and arrested with them. The exhibits at the trial were a cross, a cloth bearing religious pictures and some liturgical books.[5]

The First Popular Tribunal condemned one Luis Genís Manich to twenty years' hard labour. His crime was that of being an outstanding Catholic, of having figured as such in a number of religious associations and of having given proofs of proselytizing by propaganda carried on before July 19, 1936.[6]

A youth accused of belonging to a branch of the Federation of Young Christians of Catalonia was fined 2000 pesetas.[7]

[1] *Ibid.*, January 8, 1937.
[2] *Ibid.*, January 26, 1937.
[3] *Ibid.*, February 16, 1937.
[4] *Ibid.*, February 10, 1937.
[5] *Ibid.*, February 23, 1937.
[6] *Ibid.*, March 24, 1937.
[7] *El Día Gráfico*, April 3, 1937.

Don Luis Palomera was accused of being the editor of *Flama*, the organ of this Federation. All the evidence was in his favour, but none the less he was condemned by the Popular Tribunal to five years' hard labour.[1]

On July 25, 1937, the police arrested seven persons who were hearing Mass in a doctor's house in the Paseo del Triunfo.[2] Twelve days later, further arrests were made on the grounds that during a search money had been found which was supposed to be the proceeds of collections made for the support of Jesuits and other persons in hiding.[3]

On February 16, 1937, *El Diluvio* reported a famous trial, that of one Santiago Udina Martorell, President of a body called "Estre" which was similar to the old Marian Congregation. The charge stated that Mass was celebrated in the meeting-place of this body, which was affiliated to the Society of Jesus and supported the Falange.[4] The accused, a young lawyer who conducted himself with great dignity, spoke well and maintained his convictions firmly, made it clear that this body, like all the Marian Congregations, existed for purely religious and cultural purposes. He pointed out that it could hardly be a crime for him to be a Catholic and President of this society unless it was also a crime for Señor Aguirre, the President of Euzkadi, who was also a Catholic and a member of the congregation and had been President of an exactly similar association, to say nothing of Señor Irujo, a Minister in the Popular Front Government and Señor Ossorio y Gallardo, both of whom described themselves publicly as Catholics. Despite all this, the fiscal insisted that he should be sentenced to death. But the Tribunal was impressed and seemed inclined to absolve him. One of its members, however, who had belonged to the Congregation in his youth, had heard some militiamen say that, if he were set free, they would kill him in the street, and consequently persuaded the Tribunal to pass sentence. Sometimes, it must not be forgotten, to be imprisoned was a better guarantee of safety than to be

[1] *La Vanguardia*, April 10, 1937.
[2] *Ibid.*, July 26, 1937. [3] *Ibid.*, August 7, 1937.
[4] [*Falange Española* ("Spanish Phalanx") is the name taken to the Fascist Party in Spain.—Tr.]

set free. In the end he was condemned to ten years' imprisonment and a fine of 10,000 pesetas.

Everywhere in the Popular Front Press abundant evidence of this kind may be found. Even at the beginning of January 1938, *La Vanguardia* reported the passing of sentence by a Popular Tribunal in Barcelona upon a citizen in whose house had been found a chalice and other articles "belonging to Catholic worship, which has now been suppressed."

We have not at hand newspapers from Madrid and Valencia from which to quote similar passages, but, since in these cities the excesses committed under the Terror were greater than in Barcelona, there must be many of them. Indirect evidence in favour of this is the fact that the pamphlets issued by the revolutionaries which attempt to prove that in the Red zone there is an atmosphere of religious tolerance contain only four newspaper reports of proceedings in the Popular Tribunals—three of them from Barcelona and one from Alicante.[1] A particularly temperate writer, Melchor de Almagro Sanmartín, reports this significant fact which occurred about the middle of August 1936.

> "Things had reached the gravest possible point when the Home Secretary, Señor Galarza, thought it advisable to announce to the reporters that, as in Madrid alone 20,000 persons had been illegally executed (15,000 of them identified and 5,000 not identified) he could no longer acquiesce in the terrible situation for which he refused to consider himself responsible. He was prepared to put a stop to such acts in any possible way, even by shooting without notice. Nothing of all this appeared in the Press on account of the express prohibition imposed by the censorship."[2]

All the measures taken, however, to prevent the nightly man-hunts and the organized attacks on private houses failed. The institution of Popular Tribunals created by decree on August 24, 1936, failed likewise. Very soon, common criminals like García Oliver were organizing from

[1] Cf. here *Das Rotbuch über Spanien*, Berlin-Leipzig, 1937, which gives numerous facsimiles of documents very much to the point in this connection.

[2] *La Guerra civil española : notas para su historia*, Buenos Aires, 1937, p. 219.

the Ministry of Justice a new juridical organization, which, by means of tribunals, prisons and clandestine cemeteries, whitewashed the so-called "revolutionary justice of the people" exercised by bandits. And this in the entire territory ruled by the Anarcho-Marxist coalition, a lasting disgrace to European civilization.

In no other city were mass-crimes so frequent and terrible as in Madrid; nowhere else were prisoners' lives so much at the mercy of incendiaries; nowhere else were people so often taken off by the hundred and ambushed and murdered on the way; nowhere else are there so many cases of collective extermination achieved with the connivance of the so-called forces of law and order. What, then, could one expect to happen when the persecution of religion began? It is in Madrid that the assassinations of religious reached their most astounding proportions. It will suffice to recall the transportation to a prison in Alcalá de Henares of that large company consisting of 133 Augustinians of El Escorial. These men were the guardians of one of the finest centres of Spanish culture, one of the richest treasuries of Spanish thought and art: some of them fell ignominiously by the wayside, while others, after their arrival at their prison, were carefully watched until an opportunity occurred to murder them.

No less violent was the persecution of Christian practice and belief among the faithful. The following evidence comes from a leading personality in the religious world, one of those who experienced something of the depths to which the persecution of religion in Madrid descended. Until the Largo Caballero Ministry fell—for ten long months, that is to say—there was no kind of security against its violence. The high command, though Communistic, continually asserted that it had no desire to wage war upon religion but it neither enforced this principle upon its followers nor used any of the means in its power to restrain them. Quite apart from the outrages committed by uncontrollable gangs, the Press, though strictly controlled and censored, launched periodical attacks against persons and institutions because of their religious character. These would be quickly followed by a general wave of persecution, in which there would be new victims, both among the clergy and the laity: this persecution, naturally, would not be reported in the Press. Repeated enquiries produced lists of parents' associations, of members of Catholic Action, of confraternities and of Christian youth-groups; by these means the revolutionaries succeeded in exterminating an enormous number of Christian men and women without bringing any of them before the Popular Tribunals.

There is a tragic similarity, then, between the persecutions in Madrid and in Barcelona, which should be noted by those who have read the shameless allegations of the "Catholic" propaganda disseminated in Spain and in foreign countries by the International Red Auxiliary and by the Government of the Popular Front. Its most effective publications have been two pamphlets, the format of each of which is as impressive as its contents are base, dealing with the Basque question and with the evidence of the group already referred to, consisting of a few priests (two of them very well known in Madrid) and some self-styled "Catholic writers". The type of evidence used is that of a few poor nuns who, in order to save their lives, were forced to remain in the power of the Reds and are understood to have declared that they were "happy" among them. The pamphlets are addressed to "Catholics and Christians" all over the world. Not content with exploiting the myth of "churches converted into arsenals, barracks and fortresses of the rebellion", they aim at nothing less than persuading the world that "no Catholic has been persecuted as such in Republican Spain", and that under the Republic "persons professing every kind of belief, including priests, religious and Christian laity, live together in the utmost safety in an atmosphere of the greatest respect."

"These Christians, priests and religious", continues the passage, "are on our side. In all the territory held by the Republic not a single trial has taken place, not a charge has been preferred, and not a sentence passed which has had as its foundation the religious activities, ideas or beliefs of a single Spanish citizen. Nobody, absolutely nobody, can honestly maintain the contrary or furnish evidence which will prove such an assertion."

This affirmation forms part of the "Catholic propaganda" issued from Red Spain in June 1937. With it may be contrasted some clear and irrefutable evidence to the contrary, produced after the publication of this propaganda, at a time when "democratic order" and a "new religious tolerance" were firmly established, and, according to a Government organ, the faithful were allowed to be publicly present at private worship performed in the interior of their houses!

(1) On December 7, 1937, Tribunal No. 1 of Madrid sentenced a printer's employee named Andrés López Díaz to eighteen months' imprisonment for having worked in the offices of *El Debate*[1] and for having belonged to the Catholic Printers' Syndicate, which under the Republic was a perfectly legal body. On the following day this sentence was attacked in *El Sindicalista*, which asked the Minister of Justice, Señor Irujo, a question which the Anarchists who are members of the C.N.T. must have thought illogical: "Is it a crime to be a Catholic?" The Minister in question, though himself a Catholic, answered that for the moment he could not give a reply one way or the other.

(2) *La Vanguardia*, on April 13, 1938, printed a telegram from Madrid which described the arrests of various persons of right-wing opinions carried out on the preceding day. One of these was a certain Rosa Carbonell, a member of the political party called Renovación Española, on whom were found some religious medals, tied with bows in the monarchical colours, and a cross.

(3) During the few days for which the Reds held Teruel, out of the sixty-five priests and religious found there on their entry (January 6, 1938), twenty-seven who went out into the Republican zone from the city were assassinated by the Reds before they were outside the suburbs. This information comes from an official *communiqué* printed in *L'Osservatore Romano* on March 24, 1938.

After such striking contradictions between facts and propaganda, one would hardly think that imagination could create anything more repulsive. Yet there are worse things to record than these.

[1] [Before the Revolution, this was the leading Catholic daily paper. —Tr.]

The preface of one of the above-mentioned pamphlets, which is signed by a Madrid priest, is principally composed of a number of statements made at a meeting of the International Red Auxiliary. It is through the intermediacy of a priest that the Church's persecutors make this solemn declaration:

> " Catholics and Christians, one and all: take this and read it, for it is the truth.
>
> " *Our hands are free from Christian blood.*"[1]

It is perfectly clear, then, that the terrible acts of the revolutionaries, which were represented by propagandists as being spontaneous and uncontrollable, were in consonance with the so-called judiciary activities of the only institution legally competent to administer justice and established by the Madrid Government, by a decree dated August 24, 1936. These public Tribunals, on the one hand, like the militia, police and expert gangs on the other, treated as crimes the practice of worship even in the privacy of the home, the possession of articles with religious significance, membership of Catholic associations, the showing of charity to priests and religious—and even, indeed, the simple fact of being a Catholic, or of having taken part in Catholic

[1] The pamphlet is called *Religión y fascismo*. On the cover are the words " They burn, rob and assassinate—in Thy Name " ! An illustration shows a countrywoman kneeling before an historic wayside cross ! The whole is published by the National Executive Committee of the Spanish Red Auxiliary (June, 1937). The preface (" Words by a believer ") is signed by " Juan García Morales, priest."

Das Rotbuch über Spanien publishes (p. 58) a facsimile of the title-page of the book *El Cristo Rojo* (" The Red Christ ") written by the same priest and published in 1935 by the Bolshevik house of Castro, in Madrid. On this title-page is an illustration entitled " Image of the Sacred Heart which the revolutionaries of Membibre carried to the barricades, with the label which they affixed to it." The label reads: " Red Christ. We respect this because it belongs to us." The theme of the Red Christ, which inspired the speeches of García Morales, was exploited long before the Revolution. Like master, like pupils. In a Dutch paper (*Katholieke Illustratio*, August 26, 1937), James Murphy, a writer who spent the first five months of the Terror in Madrid, affirms that he saw at the entrance of a famous church a large statue of the Child Jesus dressed as a Communist soldier and a poster at the side which read: " I am a convert to Communism because the Church has deceived me."

Cf. also the pamphlet *El Catolicismo en la España leal y en la zona facciosa*, published by the " Servicio español de información " (Madrid, Valencia, 1937).

activities, non-political in character, before the outbreak of the Revolution.

Motives and pretexts for persecution have been found in the discovery of a person's name on the list of members of a Catholic association or as a subscriber to charitable or religious objects, of receipts for sums given for such purposes, of personal or professional relations, or family ties, with priests or religious, of photographs of popular or private religious functions or of Catholic friends. Each of these has on occasion sufficed to bring upon those concerned condign punishment ; and the more open and active the profession of faith, the intenser has been the persecution and the more severe the penalty.

No pity has been shown to those who refused to reveal the names and hiding-places of any priests or religious with whom they were in contact, especially if these were personal relatives. In Gracia, a suburb of Barcelona, the mother of a priest was assassinated for refusing to betray her son. In a dramatic description of a Madrid Tribunal published by a French writer may be read an account of how a father was sentenced to death for having a son in a seminary ;[1] another father was similarly condemned at Constantina, in the province of Seville, for having a son who was a priest. There have been frequent cases of the assassination of the sisters or servants of *curas* because they have refused to reveal their whereabouts, of which in fact they were ignorant. The *ecónomo*, or administrator, of the Church of the Sacred Family, the famous modern Barcelona church built by Gaudí, died of cancer some weeks after the outbreak of the Revolution. Before he could find a refuge in which to lay his head for the last time, he had to perform a regular Odyssey. Finally, he found a humble resting-place in the house of a poor woman. After his death it was discovered that she had given him shelter and she was murdered.

A few other cases of persecution of the laity may here be cited.

At Sabadell there lived a genial physician, Dr. Fernando Sotorra—an exemplary citizen, a great promoter of culture

[1] A. Zwingelstein : *Au pays de la terreur rouge* (Editions Alsatie-Paris), pp. 197–205.

among the people, President of the Catholic Academy founded by Sardá y Salvany during the First Republic. Few men in that town enjoyed such prestige and affection, and he can hardly have suspected that he had an enemy in the world. One day, at dusk, he was " called for ". His wife was fearful; but he set her fears at rest by telling her that the call was from a patient. Guessing the truth, she clung to him and tried to prevent him from going; whereupon the militiamen struck her, tore him away and flung him into the car which took him away to his death.

At Tarrasa there was a mass-assassination which alarmed even the Red authorities. One of the victims was a lawyer, Dr. Francisco Badía, a man of simple character and energetic habits who had taken a considerable part in the recent liturgical renaissance. Dr. Badía was traced to his house in the country and arrested while sitting with his wife and seven children at his own table. He went with his captors, after raising his eyes to the Sanctissimum, reserved in his little chapel, where, during the first days of the Revolution a number of Catholic neighbours and refugees had fortified themselves by hearing Mass.

At a crossroad near his house he saw a number of other victims and understood what was in store for him.

" Why do you want to kill me ? " he asked. " I have never been a Fascist."

His captors were silent.

" Then I understand," he said quietly. " It's because I'm a Catholic. I understand now. Let's get on with it."

One must have known him to imagine his tones of quiet conviction, to see the happy look in his eyes as he prepared for his last journey. The truth afterwards came out. Four days before the outbreak of the Revolution he had taken the chair at the first of a series of lectures on the Social Encyclicals which was given to an audience of about a hundred young members of Catholic Action.

In the house of a devout Catholic woman, near Vich, a search revealed a paper with vague indications of what seemed to be the hiding-places of some nuns. In order to compel her to betray these nuns, her persecutors shut her up in a room and told her that they would kill her children, the eldest of whom was only fifteen. So they brought the children to her one by one; and, immediately after each visit, and each of her refusals to betray the nuns, a shot was heard below in the courtyard. Despite her grief, she never wavered in her constancy and in the end her persecutors gave up the attempt, whereupon she found that the murder of her children had only been simulated in order to frighten her into making the betrayal.

A striking scene took place in the chalet owned by a staunchly Catholic family in the Barcelona suburb of Gracia. The mistress of the house, a widow, was a social worker among the poor. Her eldest daughter, a fortnight before the outbreak of the Revolution, had taken the habit as a nun; almost all the priests who had been present at the ceremony of her profession had been assassinated. In her chalet she had given refuge to a score of nuns belonging to the institution which her daughter had entered, and here they had carried on their conventual life. But the night before it was searched the Mother Superior had had some intuition of what was to come and the nuns had vacated the chalet. At three o'clock on the next afternoon the searchers came, to find their birds flown. The only arrests they could make were those of a son and a son-in-law and these they shot in the street outside. The son, a man of twenty-nine, met his death bravely, crying for the pardon of his murderers. The victims were ordered to shout: "Long live the F.A.I.!" Their only reply was: "Long live the Christian religion! Hail, Christ the King!" Thus they fell witnessing to their faith.

Some weeks later the lady of the house was found in the home of some relatives, where she had taken refuge. She escaped arrest by showing the death-certificates of the earlier victims. A few days later still this house was again invaded by revolutionaries looking for a priest who was said to have entered it to hear confessions. Again the lady produced the proofs which showed that she had already sacrificed two lives to revolutionary fury. It was useless: they only demanded the surrender of the priest more insistently. So she told them plainly: "I will not give him up: you will come in only over my dead body." This particular group of revolutionaries not being proof against such courage on the part of a woman, the priest had time to escape.

The parish priest of Riudecañas, near Reus, was arrested with six youths who were among his parishioners. Before they were shot, the priest raised his hand and said to the militiamen :

" Grant me a few minutes' grace so that I can absolve these boys ; they will want to prepare to die for Christ's sake."

He turned and spoke to them and gave them his blessing ; then aligned himself with them and said to the militiamen :

" Now we are ready : you can shoot."

This narrative was related by the driver of the car which had brought the victims to the place of their execution. So deeply was he moved by the scene that he declared he would never again be present at so barbarous a murder.

In one of the largest towns in Catalonia a doctor, whose kindness to all had made him universally beloved, was imprisoned for three months, and the Revolutionary Committee allowed him to go out daily, visit his patients and return to prison. But, in the end, he was taken to the cemetery to be shot, together with another layman—a stone-mason—and two priests. The two priests—one a rector and one the curate of another parish—had for many days been prepared to die. The doctor died with a Crucifix in his hands to the honour of God and the Church.

A few more typical cases of this frenzied persecution remain to be related.

Doctor Melchor Pou, of the Church of the Conception at Barcelona, had recently united a couple in matrimony ; the discovery of this fact by the revolutionaries cost him his life. It is said that at Aznalcollar, in the province of Seville, all who had been married in Church since the beginning of the Republic were condemned to death.

A few weeks before the outbreak of the Revolution a French Bishop performed the marriage ceremony for two Spanish friends in the chapel of a country house. When the home of the newly married couple was searched, a photograph of the ceremony was discovered. The young husband was brought before the Committee's tribunal and shown the photograph, in the centre of which the Bishop naturally figured, and also a letter accepting the invitation to marry them, in which he mentioned two Catalan Bishops, the Cardinal-Archbishop of Tarragona, and the Bishop of Solsona.

" What a fellow this must be, to have two such Fascists as friends ! " remarked someone on the Tribunal ; and they demanded that his whereabouts should be told them. On being informed that he was a French Bishop, they were furious and sentenced the young man to death. But by a fortunate chance, on that same night, he escaped ; and after some weeks of wandering in the mountains, reached France.

In the New Cemetery at Barcelona, a poor woman was seen weeping for the death of her son. One of his workmates in the factory had been heard to say : " Silly creature, he goes to Mass every Sunday. This sort of fellow does more harm than a hundred priests. They ought to be finished off."

On the next day he was shot. He was eighteen.[1]

It was seldom that the relatives of victims could obtain permission to give them burial ; to wear mourning for them was dangerous and more so still to mourn them openly. In the cemetery of Olesa de Montserrat, the sister of the parish priest, who had been assassinated, was found by a militiaman weeping for him.

" What are you crying about ? " he asked her.

"About my brother's death," she answered. "You wicked people have killed him."

A shot was fired—and she wept no more.

When the families of the victims intervened to save them, the result again and again was that women and girls were brutally attacked, and often imprisoned and killed. Even the smallest children were not exempt from this kind of vengeance ; sometimes they were even murdered in their parents' arms. This applies to the south and a great part of the east coast of Spain, as well as to a few towns in the

[1] Antonio Pérez de Olaguer : *El Terror rojo en Cataluña*, Burgos, 1937.

central area. Official accounts give evidence of the most shocking kind. One of them only shall be quoted.

A lady who lived in a large city was well known for her generosity and readiness to help any good work. When the persecution began she fled with her children, but she was unable to take with her a baby grandson, hardly a year old, who was a delicate child and had been staying with his nurse at a house in the country. The militiamen went there in search of the family, and, finding that they had all escaped, seized the child, shook it roughly and said: "Oh, if only you were a couple of years older!" On the next day they actually came back to take it away. Fortunately the nurse and the neighbours were able to save it, but one day that child will know how nearly it came to losing its life because its parents and its grandmother had contrived to escape assassination.

CHAPTER IX

THE LIVES OF THE PERSECUTED CHRISTIANS

How, we may now ask, did Spanish Catholics behave in the midst of such tyranny and oppression?

Facts and incidents without number have been reported which testify to the courage and dignity with which they upheld their Faith and gave the world the noblest of examples. Besides listing innumerable martyrs, the records of the persecution show that still larger numbers defended and confessed their Faith but were not called upon to die for it. Catholic life during the entire period might be described as one huge continuous act of confession and defence of Christianity. Could the whole of the immense store of information available under this head be published the admiration of the world would know no bounds. And it is only when peace brings a new tranquillity that we shall realize the full extent to which the virtues of charity, courage, devotion, self-discipline, serenity and radiant faith have shone forth in Spanish Catholics of every age and class, and enabled them with heroic fortitude to bear afflictions and face perils without number.

The very reasons given by the revolutionaries for their crimes, the very information published by the syndicates and tribunals furnish some idea of the tenacity with which Divine worship, when forbidden in public, continued to be practised secretly, of how the sacraments continued to be administered clandestinely in private houses, and of how Masses were said in such conditions, with constant risk of spying and informing by caretakers and servants and liability to be interrupted at any moment by loud beatings on the doors with the butt-ends of rifles.

Let us here pay a tribute of homage to the dauntless courage of clergy and laity alike, vying with each other in fervour to do honour to God and find comfort in the Communion of Saints.

O wonderful moments of Divine solitude and Divine simplicity when Mass is being said in the intimacy of the home with a fervour seldom known in times of prosperity! O memorable communions, in which the humility of the creature is united as never before with the Word made flesh Who dwells among us! O sacrilegious invaders, burning with lust to uproot the Faith from homes which have become temples for God's worship! O young men and maidens, who have become true ministers of the Church, fervent in the diaconate of an invisible Divine service, going from house to house, from prison to prison and from town to town, bearing with ingenious subtlety the sacramental Presence. O woods and mountains, ruined hermitages, lonely and remote houses that can witness to the devotion of fugitive Christians and their ministers, as they honour their Lord with a Franciscan joy uniting their praises with the unquenchable songs of His creatures! O priests and faithful laity, who have known the heroic satisfaction of remaining true to God amid such danger, have you not become the palpitating heart of the martyred Church, the invisible city of God, the temple of living stones anointed with the chrism of persecution? Are you not the royal priesthood, the elect race of the apostolic ages reborn, the communion of the Saints re-enacting the Passion of the Lord, aiding Him by your sufferings in body and in spirit to bear the Cross to His Calvary, where He effected our redemption and that of all the agonizing world?

Truly this Christian nation—and never has Spain better merited the name!—has done marvellous things. Never, even when persecution was at its height, did Spanish Catholics abandon their churches; when their churches went up in flames they carried away from them all they could and carried on unperturbed the tradition of Divine worship. Let us consider some detailed narratives.

Here, for example, is a young mother who has had to flee from a great city on the very day on which her newly-born child was to have been baptized. It is on the Friday of the first week of the Revolution that she finds a little church near the frontier where the sacrament can be given ere the priest goes into hiding and the family escapes over the hills into France.

Another young wife, with her young children, is evacuated with them from Madrid, leaving her husband in the prison where for ten long months he has been languishing. He can write very little to her, but she understands what he means when he says:

"Don't worry about me. I can keep going all right with the *bread* I get every day."

By means which it is difficult even to imagine, he has been able, even while in prison, to contrive to communicate daily.

A number of Boy Scouts, accompanied by two chaplains, were surprised by the outbreak of the Revolution in the extreme north-easterly limits of the country, just as they were preparing to embark upon a difficult climb in order to hear Mass on the Pica de Astats, the highest summit (10,660 feet) in the Catalan Pyrenees, where they also hoped to plant a Cross. Undeterred by events in the world below them, they made their ascent, and on the Tuesday of the first week of the Revolution, when the churches in the towns and villages below them were being burned and pillaged, they made their communions on those heights. The Cross was duly planted on the spot where their Mass was said, and, though attempts have been made to remove it, not one of them has succeeded.

The parish priests were by no means always deserted by their flocks, even under the greatest peril. At Pobla de Segur, Father Tapias, whose life had been spared by the local Revolutionary Committee, was taken into the public square by a gang of strange militiamen to be put to death. His parishioners hastened there to try to secure his freedom, but without avail. He begged his executioners to allow him to die wearing his cassock, said farewell to his flock, gave his forgiveness to his murderers, and, when all this was done, said: "Now fire."

This will be a suitable place to describe how the venerable Basilica of Montserrat escaped the destruction by fire which the impious revolutionaries had destined for it. To attack that great and revered monastic mountain settlement, with the five hundred inhabitants or more who were to be found there in the summer, was a feat the idea of which strongly attracted the more daring. On the first Tuesday of the Revolution, July 21, 1936, a car-load of Anarcho-Syndicalist emissaries visited the monastery to spy out the land. They did no immediate harm ; and, that night, while in the distant plain beneath the monastery one could see the flames rising from the village churches, the traditional *Salve* and the popular *Laus perennis* were sung as usual in the Basilica by monks and choir. On the following day the usual Masses were heard with a special emotion. Soon afterwards it began to be noticed that groups of revolutionaries were dribbling in. About midday there arrived four lorry-loads of Anarchists and Syndicalists, from the notorious La Torrasa, well provided with the wherewithal for their crimes. Three of the lorries drew up in front of the steps leading to the hotel nearest the Basilica, while the fourth went on to the station. From it dismounted an Anarchist carrying a parcel. Providentially he saw a workmate passing, accompanied by his mother, and stopped to speak to him. The mother, a good woman who was spending a few days here with her son, overheard a few words of the conversation ; it appeared that the Anarchist was about to fling some bombs into the church as a signal for his companions to begin a general attack upon the monastery. Without hesitating a moment she went up to her son and reproached him for having anything to do with such a man. Then she turned to the Anarchist himself.

"And how dare you and your friends come and burn Montserrat ?" she asked. "Don't you know that it belongs to all of us Catalonians and that the Black Virgin is our own mother ? Don't you see, you wretched fellow, what a crime it is ? Not only will God not forgive you but everybody will revile you for it ? Get away from here, and if you have any love for your own mother, respect ours—for she's yours as well."

So earnestly did the good woman speak that she actually managed to make an impression upon him. He turned away and rejoined his companions. Following him, she heard him talking to them. He seemed to be wavering; the others to be urging him on. While they were still talking a member of the Catalan Parliament came up, together with a picket of the Mozos de Escuadra, which had been detailed to take official possession of the Monastery in order to defend it. Had it not been for that brave woman they would have arrived only in time to see the Basilica burning.

The monks made their escape, not without experiencing some dramatic moments, which the Abbot faced with singular calm. Since then, however, more than forty have perished, victims of the monk-hunts which took place in Barcelona and in other towns which gave them refuge.

A local Revolutionary Committee arrested a girl of lowly station who belonged to one of the committees of Catholic Action.

"Do you still believe," the President asked her, "in this God who says nothing and never comes to His own defence even when His images and temples are burned and His ministers killed?"

"Which is the more important," she replied, "an image or a person?"

"A person, of course," said the President.

"Well then, listen to me," she answered. "Jesus Christ allowed Himself to be persecuted, crowned with thorns and nailed to the Cross without defending Himself. So it's not surprising if He is silent while His images are being burned. He permitted Himself to be tortured like this because, while the world was persecuting Him, He was redeeming the world. You are among His miserable persecutors; and if He is silent while you destroy and kill it is because He is pleased to prolong His sufferings."[1]

Many are the examples of such womanly courage manifested in face of the enemy. Many and varied, too, the emotions engendered by the persecution. Emotions of the faithful who, knowing that what they most revered would infallibly perish, have preferred to carry out the work of

[1] Cf. Juan Estelrich: *La Persécution religieuse en Espagne,* Paris, 1937, p. 96.

destruction themselves, venerating the very things they destroyed. Emotions of those who, at the risk of their lives, have rescued the Sacred Host and passed even through flames with their precious burden till they could place it in the hands of some fugitive priest or reverently communicate it to others in communions of indescribable fervour, recalling the most moving scenes of the persecutions of the early Christian era.

Go anywhere through the countryside, over mountains, into towns and villages—and you will find Christians living the same hidden life, deeply rooted in Christ, in the same spirit of fervent worship, happy to be serving God in the joy of sacrifice, ready to live or to die for His sake.

Only now have many believers discovered that faith is the sole invincible force of human life and that sacramental worship is beyond all compare the most inspiring form of communion with God. Almost in the course of a single day the churches were destroyed or profaned and every kind of Divine worship was proscribed ; immediately, spurred by a superhuman yearning, there sprang up the eager determination that, at all costs, Divine worship should never cease. Such was the source of the will to worship which manifested itself in the hearts of these persecuted Christians. What has still to be told is the story of how the hidden current of communion and apostleship made its way along its underground course, so that, when only a few days had passed, the Church was once more in possession of her full life and vigour.

Brethren in the faith sought each other out, gathered together, found priests by stealth, helped them to safety and with their aid quickly formed mobile communities for secret worship.

Any man known to be a priest became a treasure without price, to be protected at whatever cost. In this way the sick still received the Sacraments, newly born children were still baptized, marriages were still celebrated ; and the possibility that these rites would at any moment bring death to those who took part in them gave them a spiritual intensity hitherto undreamed of. Many a Catholic will remember to the end of his li e the day when, walking through the street, he met a friend and there ensued a whispered dialogue, inaudible to the passers-by—his confession. When a visit to his house, at any hour of the day, brought the longed-for Bread of Life. When the presence of a single stranger sufficed to turn his house into a church, giving life a new and Divine meaning and more than recompensing him for an act of charity.

Already we know of numerous providential encounters of one terror-stricken priest with another, when in solitary places each recognized the other and made what might well be his final confession. So fervent were such encounters, so great was the eagerness of these Christians for their sacramental life, that their persecutors took advantage of it to seek out and kill the ministers of God. Cases are known where they simulated religious zeal, and begged the faithful to find them a priest who would come to attend a sick man : the priest duly found, the persecutor did his work, and one more name was added to the roll of Spain's martyrs.

It may be imagined how in years to come the religious life of the country will be stimulated by the exchange and narration of their experiences by those who for months lived, as it were, the life of the catacombs—not indeed literally below ground, but in woods and fields or in their own homes.

Masses would be said secretly by fugitive celebrants, using an ordinary table or some other piece of furniture in a back room ; or on some large stone picked up in a field and carried to a secluded corner. There would be no ornaments, no missal, an ordinary drinking glass and some household bread. Sometimes Mass would be celebrated round a table, so that, in case of a surprise invasion, the Divine love-feast would appear to be an ordinary meal. Occasionally celebrations were held in caves, at dead of night—caves hallowed for ever by the Real Presence of Christ in the Sacrament of the Altar.

During this time of extreme secretiveness and precaution, the position of the head of a household acquired a new virtue and a new dignity. For to the head of each Christian household fell the responsibility and the honour of being zealous for the Lord's house and for the preservation of articles used in Divine worship. Stories remain to be told of how devout women performed, as it were, the office of deaconess, manifesting their devotion and love in their care for places and articles dedicated to the worship of God in the Holy Eucharist or in the administration of the Sacraments. Many such Christians as these could give vivid descriptions of the emotions with which they have experienced all the sanctifying efficacy of the presence of Jesus Christ, the Light of the World, shining in the darkest corners of houses and of souls newly converted into temples of God.

Imagine how many imperishable memories have been created in the houses of men and in solitary country haunts by events such as these. "Our Lord has been here," the witnesses of them will say; and the saying will be transmitted as a tradition to their descendants. They will show the places which have served as churches, and the tables, glasses and other articles which, having once been used for their sacred purpose, will be set apart and preserved from common uses for ever.

A few typical incidents of this aspect of the persecution of religion may now be given.

A distinguished lady belonging to the Consular corps of one of the Hispano-American republics saw to it that facilities for religious worship were not lacking in the Legation of her country by taking in a Dominican missionary who had shown extreme heroism in ministering to persecuted Christians in Madrid. For the celebration of the Mass this lady chose the best flagon that she could find among her plate; now that she is no longer in Spain she has had a case made specially for it and counts it among her most precious possessions. Another lady, still unhappily in Madrid, gave this same religious a particularly finely worked handkerchief for use at Mass; it must by this time have been used at many thousands of communions. Once Madrid is liberated she hopes to receive it back again and hand it down as a relic of the persecution.

Some of the cases of the celebration of Divine worship in secret have been almost miraculous. At the beginning of November 1936, in the heart of the diocese of Gerona, a religious who had taken refuge in the town of B—— was betrayed by a woman who lived near, but escaped to a neighbouring forest. With seven other fugitives he lived for some time in a cave. In other parts of the forest twenty refugees were hidden, nine of them priests, who had brought chalices and other articles from their churches. Gradually this little colony began to organize its new existence with the aid of a few country-people who brought food and kept a discreet watch around. They could hardly see the sun from their caves ; to get water they had to make a journey of three-quarters of an hour ; throughout a cold, wet winter they had no bed other than a little straw. Yet every night nine Masses were said in the darkness to the honour of God. On Sundays, a few country-people would come from the outlying districts and return to their farms before dawn. This continued until June 1937.

In the large cities, and particularly in Barcelona, this type of life quickly became normal. Both clergy and laity took part in its organization. To search for fugitive priests, to find homes for them, to place them where there had been no kind of facility for Divine worship, to provide for them by means of the generosity of the faithful, themselves also in need—all this was a labour of true love and at the same time a highly exacting one. Some who engaged in it actually died of the privations in which it involved them. But more than a hundred fugitive priests were discovered by this means—all of them in the most deplorable of plights : some of them sleeping on benches in the streets, or employed as newspaper-sellers, as street merchants or in other menial tasks.

In such detail was secret worship organized that the Canon of the Mass and the short rituals of the sacraments were circulated in cyclostyled typescript and clandestine registers of baptisms and marriages were kept and collected. Workers were soon found to make chalices and *capsæ Domini* for the Sacred Host ; and nuns and other women embroidered linen and vestments or made hosts with their own hands. There were no holy oils to be had in the stricken regions but means were found of procuring them from other dioceses, so that Extreme Unction, as well as Holy Baptism, could be administered.

If there were numerous groups of men who went from

place to place profaning and destroying the churches, there were others, hardly less numerous, raised up by God to restore them. Everywhere they went on their mission of comfort and restoration—to hospitals, where they cheered the dying ; to prisons, where they visited those condemned to death ; to ruins and rubbish-heaps, whence they salvaged articles and fragments of articles used in worship ; to abandoned chapels, some of them on mountain-tops, where they celebrated expiatory Masses and saved treasures which had not been wholly destroyed.

It is calculated that in Barcelona more than two thousand Masses were celebrated in secret. And it may be imagined how often the Rosary was said—not on beads, but on the fingers—and with what loving skill the faithful improvised crosses and found substitutes for the medals which had been torn from around their necks. Sermons were often preached at these Masses and study-groups were re-formed, their favourite theme being charity as taught in the Gospels and the writings of the Apostles. Such was the life of this heroic, suffering Christian people.

Never before has Spain seen so ardent and authentic a manifestation of Catholic Action, carried out in such intimate co-operation with the ecclesiastical hierarchy. Seldom can the Pope have spoken from such depths of love as when he addressed these his children so far from him yet so intimately united with him ; seldom can the blessing of our common Father have been carried so directly yet so invisibly to souls prostrated in a darkness which that blessing illuminated. A member of the Hierarchy brought to him one of the simple, improvised chalices which had been used by the persecuted Christians in Barcelona ; never, he records, had he seen the Holy Father so profoundly moved.

It is in the prisons, however, that future chroniclers of the persecution will find the material at once most instructive and most striking. It is certainly the first time in history that the prisons of any State have been completely emptied of their criminal population and filled with persons whose only crime was to have acted as honourable men and women. Prison life became something quite new and acquired the spiritual atmosphere of Spanish Christianity ; in that atmosphere have flourished the most edifying examples of the persecution.

As is well known, the first of the new inmates of the prisons were the soldiers and civilians involved in the defeated Army rising, and with them were political prisoners, citizens of all classes who had taken no part in the insurrection and the great body of those whose only crime was their religion. All such—those who fought against the Revolution and those who were only its victims—found a common bond of brotherhood in the confession of their common Faith.

Amid their physical sufferings, in the miserable conditions of their confinement, with the threat of still greater sufferings or of an early death hanging over them, herded together as they were in abnormal circumstances and often under brutal gaolers, their fervent colloquies and the ardour of the fellowship of their sufferings brought them together as the early Christians must have been brought together—clergy and laity uniting in acts of worship, in tranquil collective prayer, sometimes even in cautious and impressive celebrations of the Mass, which was their supreme consolation.

The prison-boat *Uruguay*, to take one outstanding example, was full of political prisoners who, after summary trials in which revolutionary rancour denied the defence full expression, had been condemned to death. There was always a priest available to assist them in their last hours, for priests were among the condemned; together confessor and penitents went to their deaths, resplendent in the halos of their victorious Faith.

Many of the intimate scenes which took place in those prisons have yet to be related in full. That early morning scene, for example, in Montblanc Prison, when from behind the grille a cardinal gives his blessing to a group of his priests and pronounces those sublime words:

> "Cherish nothing more that is purely human; have no more thoughts of conflict or of passion; let nothing be in you but charity—love to God and love to your fellow-men."

Or a scene in Barbastro prison, an oasis of primitive Christian legendry: priests and religious grouped around their

Bishop, who had been condemned like themselves, finding comfort in reading and meditating upon the Acts of the Martyrs—a scene in one sense reminiscent of monastic life but invested with a solemnity previously unknown. Or the tranquil homily delivered by the Bishop of Lérida to those numerous companions who were about to follow him to martyrdom. Or that scene in the most horrible of the Anarchist prison-dens, where even the guillotine was set up—the Convento de San Elías—illumined by the presence of the venerable Bishop of Barcelona, whose silent dignity impressed even those unaware of his identity.

One night, two French journalists visited a women's prison at Valencia, described by the gaoler as a model and humane prison, but whose blood-splashed corridors told their own story, while in one of its galleries alone were incarcerated two hundred nuns. The journalists were conducted to a cell in which were two nuns of their own nationality. These are their impressions:

> "Two unhappy girls are kneeling by the mattress which serves them as a bed. The elder is pale: she resembles the figure of a saint; her lips move in calm but fervent prayer. The younger, a mere child, is amazingly beautiful. Transfigured by ardent passion, her face is suffused by a supernatural light yet wet with tears. As they look up at us they resemble creatures terrified indeed, but ready to sacrifice their lives willingly rather than to sacrifice honour. The younger has her right hand wrapped in a blood-stained bandage. On the wall above her head is traced a scarlet Cross. . . .
>
> "The gaoler grunts. The journalists speak a few words of encouragement. The elder girl murmurs, in tones full of fervour, 'My God, Thy will be done!'"[1]

Many were the heroic and skilful acts of charity performed by priests in their efforts to assist the good people imprisoned in such conditions, often with criminals as their warders. When they were themselves imprisoned with them it was their unspeakable happiness to be able to comfort them by word, look and gesture. In other circumstances, it was a

[1] Ives Dantun: *Valence sous la botte rouge*, pp. 181–2.

case for vigilant and watchful zeal. Here a priest would apply for the job of cleaning out the cells so as to gain access to them and give their inmates the Bread of Life, which by extreme skill and by use of the most surprising expedients he had contrived to smuggle into the prison after consecrating it in a furtive Mass, celebrated who knows where and how. Here another priest would volunteer for other menial services or perform friendly offices which would gain him confidences and liberties from the gaolers who had not the least suspicion that he was still exercising his sacred ministry. And here, there and everywhere, priests who could do nothing more lived interior lives of continual prayer, giving themselves up to expiatory and intercessory petition and thus contributing to the peace of individual souls and to the success of the missionary activities of their incarcerated comrades.

Here may be related another story which seems to have been almost miraculous. In the so-called Model Prison, at Barcelona, were a father and a son, both of whom had been tried and condemned, the son having twice been led out to execution. A Navarran lay brother, however, one of those who made intercession their chief business, had from the first been perfectly confident of their safety. "Don't fear," he told the father, "your son will not die." A good monk, not easily given to credulity, explained the matter to us like this. "That lay brother," he said, "told me that he had commended the case to the Virgin of Estibaliz, and that the Virgin had given him her word. You ought to have known that brother," he added, "and heard him speak! He was a regular prodigy of intercession."

Perhaps only in Heaven shall we know all that went on between one soul and another, and between each soul and God, within that mass of suffering humanity liable in the twinkling of an eye to be snatched from life, languishing week after week in prisons of which the very existence was unknown to the world outside—in those subterranean dungeons, for example, in the Barcelona suburbs of San Gervasio and Sarriá, lit by not a gleam of sunshine, and so solitary that the victims immured in them had no knowledge either of their whereabouts or of the passage of time, hearing only, now and then, the infuriating sound of clocks all striking different hours. Only God's supreme gift of interior comfort could have preserved the inmates of such dens from madness.

This pallid sketch will give some idea of how imprisonment during the persecution served at once as a marvellous school in the Christian art of suffering, a heroic novitiate for a good death and an incomparable lesson in perfection of charity. Pain and death are God's most effectual missionaries.

Let us now attempt a general survey of our theme and endeavour to form some slight idea of the nature of the spiritual life lived by the persecuted Christians.

Never better than in these months have the faithful learned the living significance of the Beatitudes proclaimed by Christ in the Sermon on the Mount and come to know and prize the supernatural peace of the Communion of Saints. All of us, dispersed as we have been by the persecution, have experienced the Divine and human graces of spiritual union in prayer and suffering, which is one of the most potent forces of Christian brotherhood and which caused the pagans of old to exclaim: "See, how these Christians love one another!"

Can the devout reader imagine the course of an entire Christian year spent in the intimacy of the home, or in the darkness of the prison, with observance of the great festivals of Christ and Our Lady prohibited and with Saints' days celebrated only by inward songs of bitter pain, enlightened only by such brightness of memory and hope as could be reproduced in a clandestine liturgy?

One day we shall know what that first Christmas of the persecution was like, when the Lord was indeed re-born in every Catholic home and the Gospel story of the Nativity was re-enacted with its memories of the angelic songs and the fervent gaze of those who saw the splendour of the Star. We shall know something of that long and severe Lent, and how in certain houses Holy Week was faithfully kept and the Lord adored upon hidden Altars of Repose in an atmosphere of impressive reality. We shall know, in a word, how far those fugitive or hidden Christians were able to infuse the colour of each of the festivals into their personal lives and into their spiritual fellowship with one another.

One scene evoking an exceptional emotion must here be recalled. In one of the prisons in the Red zone hundreds of prisoners, taken out for their daily exercise, were able to convert what is usually a sullen tramp round the square into a Corpus Christi procession of silent adoration. For they knew that on the person of one of their number, a priest, the Blessed Sacrament was hidden. At that time, and in that one prison, there were over five hundred priests and religious, as well as a multitude of the faithful laity. Can ever the *Pange Lingua* have risen more triumphantly to Heaven than in that silent glorification of the greatest of mysteries by priests and people as they marched round the prison courtyard ?

The detractors of Spanish Catholicism and of the National Movement seem to have the strange idea that those of our countrymen who profess religious sentiments and are true to their faith have failed to observe the evangelical counsel of non-resistance to evil and indeed that they have encouraged and maintained an attitude of bellicosity. But these notes, like many others, and like many more yet to be written, should convince them that the most striking note of the Spanish tragedy has been its solid phalanx of martyrs ; its militia has been one, not of fighting Catholics but of Catholics who have suffered for being true to their religion.

If, to use a famous expression, every soul should be a church in little, it may well be said that the thousands of stone churches burned by sacrilegious mobs have sprung up afresh and taken on a new beauty as the living temples of souls burning with Divine love, forming among themselves an invisible City of God, praying and suffering, adoring and sanctifying, supremely active in charity and in all other virtues.

And when amid the din of persecution could be heard the voices of the peaceful militias of this City of God it was in a magnificent upraising of the most impressive of canticles.

In the Castle of Montjuich, standing high upon a rock on the outskirts of Barcelona, where dawn so often broke to the crack of the rifles of firing-parties, the prisoners lived in such serene fellowship that, without their quite knowing how, the practice grew up among them of singing each night the Rosary and the Litanies. And such was the fervour and unanimity with which they sang that the warders who heard them treated the practice with respect.

When the forty Claretian religious and novices were summoned to their deaths at Cervera they went serenely and courageously, singing a well-known hymn to Blessed Antonio Claret, their founder.

Townsfolk, numbed with terror, watched them leave; but, as the victims struck up their hymn, they lost their fear and joined heartily in praising this saintly founder who was himself more than once attacked by the enemies of religion.

CHAPTER X

OTHER MANIFESTATIONS OF THE CHRISTIAN SPIRIT

THE *Joint Letter* of the Spanish Bishops has been assailed by its detractors because it affirms that the two great motive forces of the National Movement have been patriotism and religion, which have also been the targets for the attacks of those who own allegiance neither to a country nor to a God.

The Bishops' affirmation, however, has not come as a surprise even to foreigners who observed how, at the very beginning of the War, and also as the War developed, the civilian army of the Counter-Revolution was formed; and how in such regions as Navarre the whole population flocked to the colours, thus giving a national and social character to a conflict which is less a struggle between ideas and parties than one in which vital needs, perennial traditions and the incoercible sentiments of Christian patriots are striving for the right of expression.

Within such a collective uprising religious feeling could not fail to inspire and impel an eager heroism.

This is no war-like reaction to the deeds of violence committed against God and against the Catholic Church, its ministers and its churches. This is no armed rising of a Church against those who would exterminate it.

A thousand times no: the Church suffers, pardons, hopes and intercedes, and has never failed to do so in those parts of the country from which she has not been driven by violence. The Church has been, not a belligerent, but a martyr, and has striven not with arms but with prayers. If in military encampments the patriots fighting for Spain hear Mass and recite the Rosary, and many make the sign of the Cross and communicate before going into action, the reason is that the beliefs, practices and sentiments of the

Christian religion are inseparable from their country's history and from their individual lives.

This is the secret of the emblems which Nationalist soldiers are proud to wear on their breasts and which have been treated with such ignoble sarcasm in the left-wing Press throughout the world.

This, too, will explain what some ignorant foreign journalist reported as follows : " It is often observed that, before going into action, the rebels give their soldiers something strange to eat ! " That " something " is the Lord's most sacred Body, which our faithful and devout soldiers take in the same way and for the same reason as did the leading French generals in the Great War, which ended in their victory.

If any further proof be needed of the depth of the religious sentiment in the lives of the Nationalist combatants, which at times reaches sublime extremes of heroism, it may be sought in the story of the Toledo Alcázar.

" She will sink into the ground sooner than be false to herself," wrote Maurice Barrès of imperial Toledo. The history of the Counter-Revolution has left an imperishable mark upon her. And the Alcázar, the symbolic witness of its secular history, as the Cathedral is of its Faith, was the invincible stronghold famous for those exceptional deeds of heroism which testify to the fidelity of the Toledan people.

The whole world thrilled with emotion as those heroes, half-buried beneath ruins, went through a seventy days' siege, attacked by mines, fire and machine-guns, without abating their all but superhuman vigour. Lieutenant-Colonel Pedro Romero, commander of the detachment of the Civil Guard which was besieged in the Alcázar, has described with an impressive simplicity some of his outstanding memories of the siege.

Beneath the deep vaults cut in the rock on which the Alcázar was built was a garrison of 1300 combatants, nearly four hundred women and 210 children, all sharing the indescribable privations of hunger and darkness.

Those endless nights which they passed in expectation of an imminent attack were illumined only by dim lamps fed with oil made from horses' fat. By night and by day Sisters of Mercy were at hand to lend any assistance and to tend any wounds. When the besieged asked for a chaplain to give them the offices of religion, relates the daily paper which they published, *El Diario del Alcázar*, the Republican Government sent them one for three hours, who gave them the absolution *in articulo mortis* and Holy Communion, after preaching a sermon which, as they said, " produced a moral effect upon us as shattering as the material effect of the bombs and shells." Finally, he baptized two children who had been born during the siege.[1]

After the chaplain's departure a cavalry captain, Sanz de Diego, " performed the offices of sexton, preacher, spiritual director and priest. It was the noblest and yet the most terrible mission imaginable. We had eighty dead and all received their last human tribute at the hands of this captain. He was a real saint. Again and again he missed a meal in order to give his ration to someone whose need of it was greater."

These heroes, who hardly had the time and strength to live, had yet the strength to bury their dead and time to pay them the fullest veneration. When they were asked why they did not burn the bodies they said : " Because we are Catholics." At first the burials took place in the riding-school ; afterwards, because of the increasing danger, in an old swimming-pool. They made niches with bricks and cement and separated the bodies each from the other by means of boards. Some of the burials took place amid upheavals and explosions, for even at such solemn times there was no certainty of freedom from attack. And just as, in the absence of a priest, the captain of a ship recites the prayers for the dead over one of his crew, so Captain

[1] Interview with Francisco de Cossío : *Hacia una nueva España* (Valladolid, 1936), pp. 303–15. With regard to the visit to the Alcázar of the chaplain, Canon Vázquez Camarasa, other published opinions coincide with that of Don Pedro Romero (Cf. Arrarás y Jordana : *El Sitio del Alcázar*, pp. 83–4, 173.) Louis Delaprée, who saw the Canon leaving the Alcázar, said : " I never knew what pallor in a man could be until that moment." From Paris, however, the Canon wrote an article (*Le Figaro*, September 25, 1936) which conveys not the slightest impression of the heroism of the garrison ; six months later (*Echo de Paris*, March 21, 1937) the Magistral of Madrid rendered them their due.

Sanz de Diego, solemn and imperturbable even in the most moving and dramatic of situations, never omitted to fulfil his twofold ministry of sexton and priest.

What supported these brave defenders was faith. It was on September 24, the festival of Our Lady of Mercy, Redemptress of Captives, that the first news came to hand of the approach of the army of liberation. On that day the members of the garrison, in relays, recited the twenty-four hour Rosary; and in the *Diario del Alcázar* one may read that, as the traditional observance of the festival is particularly appropriate in the present circumstances and no chapel is available for the purpose, each one of the faithful must say as much of the Rosary as he can in his own apartment. "We are all convinced," said Lieutenant-Colonel Romero, "that God is helping us. On the day of the first explosion the image of the Purísima in the Academy was left intact. Not a single splinter so much as touched it. Our Immaculate Lady was indeed our protectress. In Toledo now they have given her the name which we gave her: Our Lady of the Alcázar."

Antonio Rivera, President of the Catholic Youth Group of Toledo, and known as "the Angel of the Alcázar", composed, with the aid of some like-minded companions, this fine prayer to Our Lady:

> "We beseech thee, Mother and Lady, to implant in our hearts the firm resolution to extract from this test which we are undergoing some truly spiritual fruit. . . . We form the firm purpose to persevere in a truly Christian spirit in the virtues which we have learned or increased in this place. . . . We desire gaily and generously to fulfil our duties as citizens and to co-operate in the renovation of Spain. Pray for us, that there may be kindled within us a holy fire of love for our enemies and that all Spaniards may be joined together in brotherly union, with no thought other than the good of Spain and for sole illumination the faith of our fathers in the doctrine of Christ and of His Church. Amen."

At a later date, when suffering from machine-gun wounds, Rivera was visited by the Cardinal-Archbishop of Toledo.

"What will you do in the future," said the Cardinal to him, "if you want to emphasize the points in your speeches by waving your arms about, and you only have one arm ?"

"I shall show my audience the stump of the other arm," he replied with a gay laugh, "and it will be the most eloquent part of my speech."

On the morning after they were set free the garrison's first act was to attend a Mass said in those catacombs. When the priest was about to begin, a poor woman went up to him and begged him to take the Sacrament to the sick and wounded who were lying only a few yards from the improvised altar. At that moment a boy came up bearing a handkerchief containing consecrated Hosts, which he had been able to save from one of the churches in Toledo raided by the enemy. Then and there, amidst indescribable fervour, a Eucharistic procession was formed, and in that handkerchief, more precious than the richest of ciboria, the Holy Communion was borne to the sick and wounded. After this, with redoubled emotion, all heard that first Mass of thanksgiving—not only the garrison's survivors, but leaders of Church and State, the army of liberation, and the citizens of Toledo, who at last were able to breathe the air of freedom and peace.

Great Christians were made in those days as well as dauntless heroes.

On July 22, 1936, a boy of seventeen, son of Colonel Moscardó, the commander of the garrison, was taken from his mother, who, with her younger son, was imprisoned in a gloomy dungeon.

Two days later a tragic dialogue took place over the telephone. From the Diputación Provincial, in the vaults of which the boy was imprisoned, the militia commander made a special appeal to Colonel Moscardó to surrender the Alcázar.

"I demand immediate surrender. If you do not comply . . . I have your son in my power and I shall have him shot."

"You are neither a soldier nor a gentleman. If you were you would know that the honour of a soldier never allows him to hesitate because of threats. If you were to threaten to shoot my whole family I should not be deterred from doing my duty."

"You say that because you don't believe I am in earnest. You shall speak to your son and we'll see. . . . Bring in Moscardó."

The boy, Luis, was brought in and took up the instrument.

"Tell him," ordered the Red commander, "that unless he surrenders we shall shoot you."

"Hallo, father."

"What is it, my boy?"

"Nothing much, father. They say they are going to have me shot if you don't surrender."

"Well, you know what I think about it. If it's true that they're going to shoot you, commend your soul to God, give a *viva* for Spain and another for Christ the King, and die like a hero. Your father will never surrender—for the honour of Spain."

"Good-bye, father."

"Good-bye, my boy."

On August 14 the hostages were slaughtered. Luis was called up for execution while he was talking to his fourteen-year-old brother, who clung to him and would not let him go.

"Go to mother," said Luis to him. "She needs you. Go along, now, and give her this kiss from me."

Soon afterwards, Luis was shot near the Sinagoga del Tránsito, at the same time as the Dean of the Cathedral, Dr. Polo Benito.

On the morning of September 28, when General Varela reached the Alcázar, the squalid company of heroes heard Colonel Moscardó salute the General who was bringing them freedom and victory:

"Nothing to report in the Alcázar, sir."[1]

It would be difficult to find a parallel in modern times for this sublime story. The Red Revolution has created its own type of hero in the "dynamiter", who has emerged from the caves of Asturias, and in whose personality is

[1] The account of this moving dialogue is taken from Arrarás y Jordana, the best and most reliable publication on the subject. The accounts which appeared in the Press and in other books differ from it widely. See also Massis et Brasillac: *Les Cadets de l'Alcázar*. Paris, 1936.

concentrated the diabolic fury of the monsters of crime and death. The Counter-Revolution displays all its greatness in the story of the Alcázar of Toledo, which is already sure of a place in the history of the world.

The affirmation of the Spanish Bishops, quoted above, is based on observation of an objective kind with which all who have examined the facts will agree. The most abundant evidence for it could be given. And this would come, not only from the condemned cells of prisons and from the firing squads, where it might be accounted for by the nearness of death, but from everywhere—from camps, from hospitals and from behind the lines. It is because in all these places there is one and the same Christian life that God has been so often glorified by Christian deaths. There is no killing for Christ's sake, as the detractors of Catholic Spain have pretended to deduce from the *vivas* given by the combatants for Christ the King and for Spain : those cries mean that it is in the name of Christ, and for His sake, that men both live and die in the Spain which is defending her history, her civilization and her free, Christian future.

Already there has been collected a vast number of accounts of the deaths of those patriots who have fallen in the struggle, not one of whom died as an unbeliever. Some of these accounts are documents of great value for an understanding of the spirit in which this war of liberation has been waged. We shall quote two, which have already had wide currency in the Spanish Press.

The first is taken from the letter of an eye-witness of the trial and death of Lieutenant Javier Quiroga Posada, Commander of the ship *Virgen del Carmen*, who was betrayed by his crew and shot in company with a faithful engineer on January 11, 1937. The letter is addressed to his mother, a lady of good birth residing at Vigo. The spirit of ardent patriotism and religious zeal which shines throughout this detailed and moving story testifies to the nobility of spirit in both the martyrs.

"Where do you find the strength to be so tranquil in face of death ?" asked the religious who was ministering to the Commander.

"I find it", he replied, "in my faith in God and in Spain. When God is revered as we revere Him, death has lost its terrors."

The second letter is a farewell one from Fernando Vidal-Ribas y Torres, a youth of twenty-two, written to his parents on October 16, 1936, from the prison-ship *Uruguay*, after his death-sentence had been pronounced by a Popular Tribunal for the crime, as he says, of defending Spain and religion. Nothing could be more edifying or more inspiring than its robust and unaffected sobriety. One passage reads:

> "I have prayed to God that His will may be done. His will, then, is that I am to die. To God be the praise—and may He reign in Spain! Be sure that this is the happiest moment of my life."

Then he begs his parents to forgive any wrong he may have done them, and ends:

> "As on the day of my birth, when God gave me life, you were happy and thanked Him, be happy now because His holy will is done."

The preparation of a certain Lieutenant Columbine for death was quite exceptional. For eight days, in the *Uruguay*, he lived in continual expectation of hearing his death-sentence. Each day he received Holy Communion and was visited by his mother, his young wife and his little son, a baby of eight months. Only for a moment, when he saw the child, did his courage seem to falter. To his wife he said:

"I should never have imagined it possible to be so happy. My only regret is at your grief. But believe me, and be calm: it makes one very happy to think one is going to Heaven."

Gradually he inspired her with something of his own spirit; and towards the end, when she was going to visit him, she used to say: "I am going to see my saint."

One day he said to her:

"Listen: if one day you find yourself faced with death as I am, don't be afraid. I assure you that God will give you the same peace and joy that He is giving me. After all, it's only for a few years: we shall meet again in Heaven. I am dying for God and our country; and I am so happy that I wouldn't have it otherwise for anything."

He spent his last hours in making a rosary for his mother. When he died, it was with a smile and with the twofold affirmation of faith already described.

With a fervent and fearless cry of "Hail, Christ the King!" died in the Guadalupe fortress those noble hostages Victor Pradera, Beunza, Honorio Maura, the Conde de Plasencia—all thinkers, and all men of a deep idealism and love. It was in the same spirit that that vast legion of Navarrans flocked to the colours, abandoning their sheep-folds and leaving their houses bereft of men-folk—following, in short, their marvellous tradition of serving God, their country and their King, and honouring the scarlet béret of their forefathers, which in times of peace they keep as a relic of war and in times of war wear as a trophy. In that spirit, too, forty thousand young Catalonians, as different in every way as could be, made their way into the Nationalist camps, in threefold peril of their lives—from the persecution of the revolutionaries, from the Red spies who infested the mountains and from the enemy's bullets—to fight valiantly against those who own no country and no God.

Religion in Spain, it seems, had depths not previously plumbed. Religion has been the one universal force which has been able to give our countrymen character and nobility in the hour of their testing.

Dr. Agustín Riera was a leader of the Lliga Catalana[1] in the province of Gerona. He was a man of the firmest character and of great serenity, respected both as a medical man and as a politician in Gerona and in the neighbouring village where he resided. Despite the counsels of friends and adversaries alike, he refused to go into hiding and continued to visit his patients as of old. He seems to have had the conviction that he would lose his life; and he was ready. As though by intuition, on the very day on which he was arrested as he came out of a patient's house, he had said to his daughter—a novice who had returned home for safety—with reference to his son, a student at Cádiz:

[1] [The right-wing Nationalist Party of Catalonia.—Tr.]

"I shall most probably be killed. If you find out who has done it, tell your brother not to bear them any grudge. You will know that I have forgiven them."

And so saying, he went out to meet the death which was awaiting him.

Daniel de Ferrater, a boy of nineteen, was secretary of the Traditionalist Student Group of Barcelona. A brother of his was in hospital, dying from wounds received in the bombing of the Artillery Barracks, where he had been engaged in battle. Though the persecution was then at its height, and the churches were still burning, Daniel fearlessly brought him a confessor. His father, a retired army officer, had fallen into the hands of the POUM and been set free ; but the mob was determined on vengeance. Before he could get home, he was stopped by a patrol, which started to search him.

"There's nothing against *you*," said one of them : "it's your brother the Carlist. . . ."

Then suddenly they found on him a most incriminating document :

"What's this ? A copy of a lecture by Father Laburu ! With your name on it, too ! Well, there's no need to go any farther."

So Daniel was taken away, and soon afterwards, near Moncada, his body was found, tied to a tree, with a bullet wound in the leg and the veins in his wrists severed. So ended a life devoted to the ideal.[1]

The following story is taken from the *Avance Oficial* which deals with the atrocities in Málaga. A devout lady, who had spent her life in working for the poor, was arrested and put into prison. When they took her out to be shot and tore from her the crucifix which she was holding in her hands, she merely crossed her arms so that she might still die making the Sign of the death of her Lord. She, too, as they fired, made the twofold affirmation of faith.

In a lecture given at Brussels, the Abbé Moor tells of a *requeté* in his eighteenth year, whose hand was blown off by a grenade. The Abbé ran to his side and said :

"What is it ? Can I be of any use to you ?"

[1] Antonio Pérez de Olaguer : *El Terror rojo en Cataluña*, p. 72.

The boy showed his mutilated arm and answered :

"Make the sign of the Cross on my hand to consecrate my sacrifice."[1]

The following are extracts from a letter breathing the purest idealism. They are written by a student of nineteen named Cristóbal Riego, a volunteer at the front, to his father and mother.

> "You tell me, Mother dear, not to expose myself to too much risk, because I shall have to help you at home. But am I not fighting for our future and for the future of all Spaniards ? Yes, and much more—fighting to save all Europe, to defend Christian civilization. . . . You must be proud to have a son fighting for so noble a cause. And you will have reason to be proud if I die fighting for Spain on the battle-field and seal the motto 'God, Country, and Empire' with my blood. After all, we don't live in this world to enjoy life but to act as God commands. So the motive of our lives must be strength and virtue and that means courage and sacrifice. Only in this way can we attain our ideal, which is to die happily because we have fulfilled our duties to God."

Another young Phalangist named Formo wrote to his father in these words :

> "Don't worry about me. I am fighting only for God, our country and the things we hold dear. . . . I offer God my trials, my sufferings and my life in expiation for my sins and for the salvation of Spain. If I die fighting for God and our country I shall be satisfied, because the sacrifice of my life will have expiated my sins and those of my misguided countrymen."[2]

This same simple and ardent spirit—the spirit of a Knight of the Ideal : man, Catholic, patriot—is found in other witnesses, foreign youths, such as the Irish legionaries, who went to Spain to take part in the fight to save our Western Christian civilization. I have read some moving notes, for

[1] *Légion nationale*, February 27, 1937.

[2] Translated from H. Baldauf : *Christen im spanischen Sturm*, Saarbrücken, 1937.

example, taken from the diary of a French volunteer, worthy of the generation of Péguy and Psichari. I cannot resist the temptation of reproducing a few paragraphs from some letters written by an Italian aviator, who fell for the same ideal, to the girl to whom he was betrothed :

> "Kiss Mother often from me. Don't leave her ; and comfort her if she grieves. And you. . . . Wait with faith and confidence. Few men are given the privilege of fighting in peace-time. If I go under, I shall die happy at having lived to some purpose. . . .
>
> "At times, in the air, when we are fighting, I think of you with an intensity which is something like pain. . . . It seems to me that a superhuman force and an infinite Divine goodness are helping us in our sacred mission. . . .
>
> "The place is swarming with Russians and they have more machines than we have. These people do dreadful things. The regions they occupy are fetid with blood and decaying matter. . . . So far we have brought down 84 enemy planes. . . .
>
> "If the future is kind to me when this fierce phase of history is over, I will devote the rest of my life to your happiness. . . . Be faithful to me, if you still love this man of yours who has left you to fight for an ideal. When peace descends among men again, I shall be proud of having defended and suffered for my faith and I shall be able to love you more sincerely than before. . . .
>
> "They have asked me if I want to be repatriated. I have said 'No', for two reasons : first, because I am not afraid to stay ; secondly, because I came out to fulfil a sacred mission and I will stay here till it is accomplished, if God gives me life."[1]

Six months later, the 'plane of another aviator, Luigi Lodi, fell in enemy territory not far from Aranjuez. Nothing has since been heard of him. His wife, a doctor of medicine, a gentle, brave Christian like himself, still lives in hope of his return. Before leaving, he had said to her : "We are too fortunate : we are to give something to God." His will,

[1] *Aviazione legionaria : Lettera a la fidanzata di un cacciatore della "Cucaracha"*. (August-December 1936.)

signed at Trieste on December 13, 1936, is a heroic offering of his life and happiness for the triumph of the religion of Christ and of Roman civilization.

"Whatever news you hear," he had said to her, "don't waver: I shall come back." And her heart still mounts, on wings of desire, to join those who share her husband's ideal.

We could cite an endless number of remarkable illustrations of the sublimity of this double ideal, which cannot pale even beside the horrors of war or those lamentable excesses which at their worst surpass them.

When the Nationalist troops recaptured one of their lost positions on the Guadarrama front, they found the bodies of their dead *requetés* piled in charred heaps, the Reds having set them on fire. But among the remains they found one outstretched arm, the hand still holding a copy of *The Requeté's Book of Devotion,* open at the page headed "Recommendation of the Spirit", with which that boy had hallowed his last moments on earth.

At dead of night a detachment of Carlists were celebrating Mass when a bombardment began. No one moved: all remained on their knees at prayer. A few were killed. Their companions envied them. "What happiness", they said, "to fall for Christ and our country during a Mass!"[1]

The mothers of these brave fellows felt and spoke in the same way. The body of a youth killed at the front, at Urroz, near Pamplona, was taken to his home; and the hearts of those who bore it were full of anguish and pity for the parents. When they reached the house, there was a great silence. Then the mother kissed her son's face.

"My son," she said simply, "God grant that your blood may be the last to be shed in Spain for our Faith and our country. Long live our Faith! Long live Spain!"

It is in this way that Catholicism, free, respected and practised throughout the nation, has inspired the patriotism of the heroes of the National Movement. It is in this way that it has given sublimity to sentiments of patriotism by uniting them with religious fervour at the moment of death,

[1] From a lecture given in the Russian Orthodox Church by Dr. Lodygensky, a member of the International *Pro Deo* Committee: *Nos Frères sous la Croix en Espagne*, Saragossa, 1937, p. 18.

so that countless victims have fallen who could never have expected to be sacrificed for God and their country. The well-known saying of Bossuet has found its full realization in Spain :

" When death approaches, reason returns and vengeance is no more ; and it is then that the love of one's country awakens."

The love of one's country : yes, but, above all, the love of God.

Let us seek God everywhere. Let us see the Church triumphing in righteousness wherever a single soul is mindful of its sonship.

Let us penetrate, then, to the depths of the Red zone and we shall learn once more the providential lesson that God brings good out of evil.

One example of this is to be found in the many occasions when the heroism and the magnanimity of the victims have disarmed their persecutors' fury and touched their hearts. When evil has been met by good, even in hours of frenzy, evil has not always triumphed. In the midst of so much savagery, by the side of so many bestial acts of incredible sadism, we find frequent traces of sensibility, and we remember that good mingles with evil even in the most deformed and perverted of human souls.

It would even seem that the leaders of the persecution of religion foresaw this danger to their exterminatory ambitions and that this explains their general practice of entrusting their worst crimes to picked gangs responsible directly to themselves or to groups of men who were strangers to the locality in which they had to work and who would thus be immune against personal feelings of respect for, and attachment to, those who have done no wrong. If such an attitude reveals, on the one hand, an excess of iniquity in the organizers of the persecution, it also constitutes an implicit recognition of the greatness and beneficence of the Church, her institutions and her ministers, and also of the religious Orders, since such careful arrangements had to be made for attacking those whose spiritual and social ministry made them inviolable to those among whom they lived.

Abundant illustrations of the contagious nature of their goodness can be cited. In some places the parish priests owed their escape to the silent protection of the local Revolutionary Committees. Where the inhabitants of monasteries and convents were saved this was due to the people living in their locality. Again and again the ferocity of the sanguinary Tribunals established by Revolutionary Committees in every district was mitigated by the serene reasoning of clergy and laity who were brought before them, and, through the power of righteousness and truth, succeeded in restraining their fury.

But the most striking examples of this phenomenon will be found in the history of the early days of the revolutionary outburst. It cannot be denied that at this stage of the Revolution many deluded political idealists, completely devoid of blood-lust, joined hands with the rude mobs and the professional disseminators of hatred and perpetrators of crime. Wherever the hands of these Utopia-dazzled idealists were seen the destructive fury symbolized by the battering of doors with rifle-butts was softened by some touch of humanity.

A lady well known in Barcelona had sought refuge in the humbler house of some relations in a distant suburb. Her hosts had taken warning by events and carefully stripped their house of all that had to do with religion. Hardly had the lady settled down in her new surroundings when the ominous visitors arrived, with their brusque enquiry: "Any arms? Any signs of religion?"

"Nothing," was the reply. "You may look everywhere."

Alas, the very first cupboard they opened was full of the guest's belongings, among them many articles of devotion. She explained that she had only just arrived, and added:

"At any rate, these rosaries are the only arms I have."

The militiamen looked at her, half-amused and half-regretful.

"All right," they said. "We haven't seen anything. But do be careful. If the Murcian Anarchists come along you will all be lost."

That is a typical story and not in the least unique.

On July 19, 1936, in the stately Carmelite convent of the Barcelona suburb of Gracia, the Community Mass had just been said with the noise of battle clearly perceptible in the distance. A patrol entered. The Prioress, gracious and calm, listened to its accounts of what was happening and replied :

" If you have any wounded, bring them here : we will look after them."

There and then she ordered the infirmary to be prepared and in a few hours' time it was filled with the wounded. The patrol-leader came in to see them on several occasions and was always full of respect and gratitude. On the third day he was clearly worried about something. He asked to see the Prioress.

" You are in danger," he said to her briefly ; " you will have to get out of this. It's a bad business. Say where each of your nuns wants to go and my men will see that they get there safely."

" But what about these wounded men ? " asked the Prioress.

" We will see to that," was the reply. " You must leave them and go."

" But first," said the Prioress, " I shall have to do something very urgent, even at the risk of my life. You won't understand, but I must go into the chapel."

" Very well," replied the patrol-leader. " I'll come with you."

So, with another nun and the patrol-men, the Prioress went to the Tabernacle, took the consecrated Hosts from the two ciboria, and, with her companion, knelt and consumed them all. It must indeed have been a moving scene. The militiamen stood there, bareheaded, carrying their arms, silent witnesses of this last act of homage to be paid in that convent to the Eucharistic Presence. This duty done, the nuns left the convent, under the protection of these men, who had given them preference over their own wounded.

In a Catalan cathedral city, during the initial confusion caused by the Revolution, a priest who held a position of high authority informed a person of left-wing opinions, who was implicated in the movement, that in a certain church there was a ciborium full of consecrated Hosts which, except through his help, could not be saved. The left-wing leader effected the rescue and brought the ciborium to the priest in his hiding-place. Months later he was himself persecuted by the revolutionaries (for the moderate men of the Left have again and again been attacked by the extremists) and obliged to flee from the country. From his place of exile he wrote to the priest, saying that he was sure that he owed his salvation to the protection of God, accorded him because he had done that good deed, not without personal peril.

Sometimes the very inhumanity of the persecutors led to a reaction on the part of such of their supporters as had not yet disposed of their souls to the devil. It was in another of Catalonia's cathedral cities that a revolutionary leader told his followers that he would give five hundred pesetas for every priest in hiding that they brought him. Soon after this one of his men confided the incident to a relative, adding :

"Well, that's what he said. And I know where three priests are hidden. But it's a dreadful thing. I wouldn't think of giving them away, that I wouldn't."

The three priests escaped.

In the Asturian revolution of 1934, as in the present one, the lives of nuns were, with certain exceptions, spared : this was particularly so in Catalonia. Even in the mining regions of Asturias a few Dominican nuns managed to keep their habits until the Nationalist troops entered. The reason for this can hardly be respect for women, since many women have been murdered by the revolutionaries and others have been bestially outraged. Nor can it have been the simple fact that they were nuns, for their vocations were often insulted, their characters defamed and their habits ridiculed and sometimes put up for sale at mock auctions. A more adequate explanation would seem to be that the popular admiration for these ministering angels made the leaders of the Revolution fear that their cause would suffer if they attacked women among the most heroic that the world has known, who were revered by even the most misguided sections of the populace.

The result of this has been that, in some localities which have suffered less than others, nuns have been able to remain in hospitals and alms-houses which the revolutionaries have secularized. Here, sometimes in lay dress, they have risen above all considerations of personal peril and persevered in their ministries. It would be difficult to describe the emotions of those Christians who have been fortunate enough to come into contact with them in the hour of their need, perhaps when they least expected it, and to receive spiritual consolation, including the Bread of Life or Extreme Unction, which they desired more keenly even than essential physical attention to their ailments or wounds. None but God can know what this has meant to many militiamen who had never dreamed of encountering such truly maternal love by their beds of pain, of having their sufferings mitigated by such devoted care and of finding someone anxious to point them the way to Heaven.

In several parts of Catalonia, again, including some of the larger towns, not only have nuns remained in hospitals and alms-houses, but both monks and nuns have contrived to obtain permission to teach. One of the most distressing features of life in the Red zone is that children and adolescents are being perverted and the reverence due to childhood is forgotten. Great, then, is the blessing that must attend these heroic efforts to implant in children the seed of eternal life : silently and invisibly it will grow, under the very eyes of the enemy.

Wherever one may go, then, in the Red zone, one will find good alongside evil, pain which gives the sufferer perseverance, supernatural energy which brings strength. The necessity of being prepared for the storm, the exigences of an atheism which would destroy all religious individuality, has permitted and indeed compelled believers, including priests and religious, to enter left-wing organizations, militias and public services beneath the syndical mask or beneath the enslavement of military service. In such conditions, at the cost of many inward sacrifices, in face of blasphemy or injustice, and by means of excellence in forced labour or a skilful penetration of efficacious intervention, who can tell how many lives have been saved, how many evil deeds prevented, how many unsuspected blessings obtained ?

Imagine the quiet and sublime moments of life on the Red fronts, in which (especially in the first weeks of the War) Soviet propaganda mingled with insolent orgies, revolutionary violence and blasphemies against God. And among these revolutionaries there have been thousands of sober, patriotic Christians, whose hearts and souls were elsewhere, secure in the higher life of their twofold faith. What suffering, what heroism is to be found there, what a blessed sacrifice of continual intercession, what reparations have been made to God by interior confessions of faith, Divine worship and fervent prayer! How incommunicably those souls have become enkindled, how they must have yearned to give expression to their feelings in words and gestures, even (as in certain Saints) beyond the physical limits of which they are capable.

I have heard Nationalist soldiers describe their feelings when on various occasions, after a battle, they have recognized the bodies of companions on the other side who have died without firing a shot because they have known that the so-called enemy were men of their own fellowship and sharers of their own ideals. Here is an example of legitimate, heroic self-sacrifice, a new aspect of the mind of the conscientious objector.

Among the many heroic sacrifices in which the present Spanish tragedy abounds the most admirable are those of such youths who have been forced to serve on the side to which they are opposed and have found no way of escape from the worst humiliations and the greatest sufferings. But God has had a reason for allowing them to be kept there. Their task has been to sing His praises in the midst of organized atheism; to witness, in the midst of militant passion for the materialist revolution, to the supernatural world which lies beyond our own; to minister to the salvation of souls in a region so largely deprived of the priesthood. These youths, within the interior retreats of their souls, have prayed to God and interceded for those around them ; and, when the time has come, they have assisted men who were neither of their country nor of their faith, have signed them with the Cross and made them feel the presence of a forgiving God. How many—men perhaps misled or exploited and not fully responsible for their actions—have in the hour of death remembered the long-forgotten prayer, the face of a Christian mother, the blessing received at the hand of a priest or of a teacher ! At the beginning of May 1937, in *El Diluvio*, the most revolutionary and anti-clerical paper in Barcelona, a war correspondent described such a scene as this, and told how he, an unbeliever, helped a dying man at the front to recite a Paternoster.

"What do you want ?" he had asked him. And the hardly audible reply had been :

"Tell Mother that I am thinking of her as I die. I want to say a Paternoster and I've forgotten how !"

Many such half-uttered Paternosters, in the spiritual wilderness of the Red fronts, will have pointed wanderers back to God ; and again and again God's grace will have triumphed in those who hitherto had forgotten Him or fought against Him as though He were their greatest enemy. And many other deaths, of those who have been faithful to Him and given their lives for Him, have been nothing less than marvellous visions of the Lord, who has come down to their souls, of the Great High Priest who, without human intermediacy, has administered to them the grace they needed for a good death.

We must not bring to a close this exploration of Christian sentiment in the Red zone of Spain without pointing out some other interesting aspects of the phenomenon.

The heroism of our martyrs has often effected conversions, or, if one may use the theological term, has served their executioners as a "sacramental". Sometimes these executioners have dropped their weapons in amazement ; sometimes they have sworn to take part in no further murders ; sometimes they have become completely and fully converted.

To the story already narrated of the dying militiaman who acknowledged that he had assassinated thirty-two priests, may be added the fact that among his victims were a priest's father and two brothers. The priest gave him the assurance of his personal forgiveness and promised to pray for him. This soldier cried out before his death:

"May every one forgive me! I accept death as expiation for my crimes. Hail, Christ the King!"

Does not the reader remember the edifying death of García Atadell, that death-dealing leader who fell into the hands of the authorities in the Canary Islands, President of the Tcheka of the Madrid Fine Arts Club, who had pronounced over seven hundred death-sentences and accounts of whose Pantagruelian banquets had filled the Red chronicles of the martyred city!

Is not the reader impressed by the affirmation of the Spanish Bishops in their *Joint Letter*, that, "when condemned to suffer the extreme penalty of the law, the vast majority of our Communists have at the moment of death been reconciled to the God of their fathers. In Majorca only 2 per cent have died impenitent; in the southern regions not more than 20 per cent; and in the north perhaps fewer than 10 per cent."[1]

Another case worthy of inclusion in any Book of Martyrs comes from the *Journal d'un Prêtre* already referred to, whose author, besides being a great lover of the people, is notable for his moderate outlook and apostolic zeal. It refers to the death of Catalonia's most popular preacher, Dr. Juan Lladó, a prebendary of the Cathedral of Vich.

When told by militiamen that he was to die, he gave them a pleasant smile and thanked them.

"What!" they asked, "aren't you afraid of death?"

And the good Doctor replied:

> "No, no. If you will give me time, I will tell you why the prospect of immediate execution makes me happy. All my life long I have asked God for three chief graces.

[1] *Joint Letter*, p. 22. This observation has been criticized by M. Bernanos in his *Les Grands Cimetières sous la lune*, a book accusing the Archbishop-Bishop of Majorca of conformity with, if not collaboration in, the worst military excesses, and using the certificates of Easter Communions, which are traditional there, as in many parts of Spain, as evidence for the existence of a "White Terror"! These and other examples of anti-clerical distortion completely discount the value of the book in question.

First, for my own salvation, for this must mean most to any man; and, since I am a priest, this kind of death gives me the confidence that God will open Heaven to me. Secondly, that I may shed my blood for Jesus Christ and be a martyr; and you are going to kill me in such a way that that desire of mine is fulfilled. Thirdly, that by my death, I may save some soul—one soul only—and that that soul may go to Heaven with me and not to Hell. If among you who are going to shoot me and whom I now pardon, God can find such a soul, and I can be the occasion of his salvation, I shall die quite happily."

As he spoke, one of the militiamen, touched by Divine grace, flung down his rifle, threw himself at the feet of the priest, kissed his hand, and, in a voice trembling with emotion, cried:

"I am that soul whom you have begged of God. I ask your pardon and I will die with you for Jesus Christ's sake."

The others, infuriated, at once raised their weapons and shot both the priest and the converted anarchist.[1]

Let us now record other incidents of a different kind, in which are also revealed spiritual upheavals brought about by servants of God.

In one of the largest monasteries of Toledo, the militiamen incarcerated more than two hundred nuns. At first they did nothing but subject them to stupid mockery. They made them appear in public, and forced them to put their arms round their (the militiamen's) shoulders, and to say "These are our 'friends'." They also made them walk round the monastery courtyards, crying: "The Republic for ever, and down with the clergy!" and then abused them for not shouting louder, which they were quite unable to do. Finally, they told them to cry "There is no God!" but instead they all cried with one voice: "No, no: we would rather die!"

After some time the Prioress of the Dominican Nuns of

[1] "Evadé d'Espagne. Journal d'un prêtre" (Feuilleton 15 of *La Croix*' October 28, 1937).

the Convent of the Mother of God succeeded in mitigating the militiamen's brutality. One day she said to their leader:

"Señor Tomás, I believe that, in our chapel, the consecrated Hosts have been profaned and thrown about the floor. Would you allow me to have them?"

The leader was struck by her tone, and, as she had been exceptionally pleasant and kind to his men, he thought for a few moments and then said:

"Very well."

So she gave him a new handkerchief which she had kept for the purpose and soon afterwards one of the men came back with the Hosts, some horribly profaned, some unharmed, and these, in a communion of expiation, she reverently consumed.

A girl employed in an office had rescued a small but much-venerated image of great antiquity and hidden it in her house in Barcelona. She had also given shelter to two monks. One day, on returning from work, she found a search patrol in possession and the monks undergoing the severest examination. The leader of the patrol confronted her and asked her to confirm the identity of her guests, a confession of which he had succeeded in forcing from them.

"Don't be afraid," said one of the monks to her. "Tell them everything."

"Certainly not," she replied. "It's my duty to perform acts of charity even at the risk of my life."

The leader of the militiamen then proceeded to examine the house, and, on entering the girl's room, noticed a little box with a label bearing the words: "For consumptives."

"What is this?" he asked.

"A collecting-box," she replied. "I have had it for years; it goes to help provide a bed for poor consumptives in the Hospital of the Holy Spirit. I've gone on with it in spite of the bad times."

"Oh, so it's only for Catholics. What fanatics you are!"

"Dear me, no. Why, the very last person to have that bed was an out-and-out unbeliever and revolutionary."

"I don't believe it."

"Well, I'll explain and you'll see. We don't consider

if persons we help are Catholics or no. We do works of mercy for the love of God and we don't consider who the person is we're doing them for. We're all brothers."

"And you would take me into your hospital, if I needed it? As a matter of fact, I have had tubercular trouble."

"We'd take you just as much as we did the other man, who was a comrade of yours."

The man was impressed and would clearly have liked to continue the conversation on Christianity. But the rest of the patrol were impatient to take the two monks out to the car for their last journey. Finally the leader came out to them and said: "I will see to these people alone." They protested and tried to assert their authority, but without success. Then the leader said to the monks:

"You can go away safely. This woman has won."

They hesitated, fearing a trap.

"It's all right," he said, "I will accompany you wherever you want to go. I didn't know Catholics were like that."

He was as good as his word. The venerated image remained in the house and the girl continued to collect money for her poor consumptives.

On January 23, 1937, in Barcelona harbour, a company of one hundred and twenty nuns were on the point of embarking for Italy. They formed part of one of the large consignments of persons rescued from danger, a single one of which alone numbered nine hundred. Armed militiamen were on guard, acting as police and customs officers combined. The formalities were long and painful, especially for persons leaving their country because of persecution. Here are two interesting conversations which took place during the period of waiting.

The Superior of a convent, a nun whose seniority and manner imposed respect and sympathy, was talking to one of the militiamen.

"See how you are driving us away," she exclaimed, with feeling. "Aren't you ashamed of giving all this pain to old and feeble women?"

"We aren't driving you away," he replied. "You are going of your own free will."

"Certainly not; it is your persecution which has no respect for us, forbids us to live our lives in peace and drives us out as though we were a danger. What harm have we done?"

"Señora," replied the man, in tones of great earnestness, "in any case it's not our fault any more than yours. It's *those others* who are to blame."

"Well," she answered, "we can't discuss politics. We only do good works and works of mercy. And you are driving us away."

One of the officers of the militia had been particularly courteous; and before they went on board the Superior said to him: "We are very grateful to you. I can do nothing for you now, but I want to thank you on behalf of all of us."

"Yonder, perhaps," said the officer, looking at her gravely. And with an expressive gesture he pointed upwards to Heaven.

At this moment the man who had been previously speaking to her came up to her again. "When you see the Pope," he said, "tell him that we too have wives and children, and ask him to have pity on us."

"I shan't see the Pope," said the nun, "but I shall commend you to God."

"Yes, yes, you will see him," he replied. "Tell him to have pity on us. He is the father of all, the father of the whole human race."

CHAPTER XI

NATURE OF THE MARTYRDOM

In his moving allocution to the Spanish refugees, delivered on September 14, 1936, the Pope began by paying a tribute to the martyrs of the persecution and by extolling their greatness:

> "There is a splendour all its own which belongs to Christian and sacerdotal virtues, to heroic deeds and martyrdoms—true martyrdoms in the sacred and glorious sense of that word, martyrdoms in which were sacrificed the most innocent lives, the lives of old and venerable men, youthful lives still in their flower; martyrdoms of which the victims, in their generous heroism, have gone so far as to ask for a place in the vehicle along with those whom their executioner is taking to their death."

These words of the Pope's will always figure at the head of the annals of the persecution of religion in Spain, as an august eulogy and a prelude to the supreme definition. Meanwhile all Spanish Christians are comforted in their affliction by these words and also enriched and rewarded by the highest and most authoritative recognition that earth can give of the glory of their martyrs and confessors.

Yet in an English review of anti-Fascist views edited by Dominicans, an arbitrary interpretation was cast upon the question and doubt was thrown upon the authenticity of the martyrdom suffered by so many during the persecution of religion.[1]

Later, the Spanish Bishops expressed themselves in the same terms as the Pope, and those who cannot refrain from

[1] *Blackfriars*, September, 1936.

carping at the sublime are still seeking pretexts for invalidating their definite and authoritative affirmation :

> " We count our martyrs in thousands ; in their witness lies hope for our poor country. In the entire Roman Martyrology we should hardly find a form of martyrdom to which the Communists have not subjected our victims ; we do not even exclude crucifixion. And, in addition, there have been new forms of torture which modern invention and machinery have made possible."

This seems indeed a strange attitude to be taken by persons who would disclaim nothing so much as the name of materialist, when the very Reds who have committed these crimes have experienced and described the thrills of admiration which the heroism of the martyrs has produced upon them. Even in the frenzy of the struggle they have not been blind, as have these others, to the point of mingling political passion with blood shed in so pure and sacred a cause.

One of the leaders of the Anarchist cut-throat gangs was heard by some prisoners to say : " It is really a pleasure to kill the *curas*. They neither protest nor resist ; they let themselves be killed like lambs ; and then on top of it all they forgive us." Despite his cynicism, this man was unwittingly uttering a Biblical eulogy of the Lamb of God and of His imitators, and describing one of the most characteristic traits of the Christian holocaust, that of the pardon accorded by the victims to their persecutors.

Striking eye-witness accounts have been given of the events which took place among the captives in the Castle of Montjuich, and which were witnessed by many of the Reds on account of the frequent intervention of guards and firing-squads and the large number of hearings by tribunals. The atmosphere of that great prison was so intensely other-worldly that a number of unbelievers were converted and the prisoners' enemies were amazed to find among them neither terror nor grief. Here is one conversation which took place among many. Several militiamen remarked to a group of prisoners how surprised they were to see them going happily to their deaths.

"You see," answered the prisoners, "for us death is the beginning of a new life, the only true and happy life."

"We can't understand it!" said the militiamen. "But you certainly don't look as if you are going to die."

Sometimes the astonishment was given public expression. A Marist Brother had been condemned to death by a Popular Tribunal. Unmoved and serene, he addressed the President, pointing out how iniquitous was the persecution, and ardently defending its innocent victims and the honour of God. He ended with these words:

> "What can you do to me? Take away fifteen or twenty years of my life—that is to say, fifteen or twenty years of sufferings? I pardon you; but one day you and I and all of us shall meet before that same Eternal judge in whom you yourself believe. Unless you are converted you will receive the sentence of eternal death, which will not be a happy one like that which you are about to confer on me."

On the next day, a Barcelona newspaper reported the session of the Tribunal and eulogized the firmness and courage of which this religious gave such admirable proof.

There is another type of testimony no less revealing. Two old priests who had curacies in Berga were murdered in the cemetery of a neighbouring village. One of them gave his rosaries to a well-known militiaman so that he might give them to his sister as a souvenir: they were, however, destroyed by the rest. The bodies of both men were mutilated and destroyed, because otherwise, as the militiamen put it, "they would have been honoured as martyrs."

Their intuition did not deceive them. Here is one of many typical cases of such spontaneous veneration. A Dominican lay sister, after being outraged and tortured, was brought from La Rabassada (a sinister theatre of executions at that time) to a Barcelona hospital. She was dying; and, though an operation was performed, it was powerless to save her. In the course of the operation the surgeon's white gown was stained with blood. The nurses were about to take it from him to be washed; but he refused to give it them. "Leave it," he said—and there was a tremor in his voice—"I shall keep it; this blood is the blood of a martyr."

He was right. The martyrs of the persecution, say the Bishops, can be counted by the thousand. And, as the Pope puts it, they are martyrs in the most glorious and sacred sense of the word.

They are martyrs because they have been persecuted, condemned and killed out of hatred for the Faith and for the Church, by the enemies of God and by the Godless.

They are martyrs because they have patiently borne sufferings unjustly inflicted.

They are martyrs, because they have voluntarily accepted death for God's sake, for Jesus Christ and for the Church.

They are martyrs, because it is love, the expression of all perfection and heroism, which has been the motive and inspiring force of the sacrifice of their lives which they have made from love of God and for the salvation of their neighbours.

They have been true *witnesses* for the Faith, and "witness" is the literal meaning of the word "martyr".

To this pure spirituality from which derive the qualities of martyrdom there is decisive and documentary witness.

We might say that it is their murderers themselves who, by persecuting priests and Catholics deliberately, and with premeditation, have put their victims into the position of martyrs.

That their intention was directed against God is patent from the facts, all of which reveal a policy of extermination independent of, and standing quite apart from, the political and military events of the situation created on July 19, 1936. The war against the Church stands out as something quite distinct from the Civil War; the latter merely served as a pretext for the former and provided the appropriate moment for it to begin. All attempts that have been made to justify it have come to grief when an enquiry has been conducted into its precedents and into the facts of its dastardly consummation.

Had this not been so, priests, and Catholics in general, would have been the objects of a courteous and preventive vigilance; they might have been put under precautionary arrest and kept as hostages, in order to guarantee the authorities and the revolutionaries against their co-operation, supposed or possible, in any reaction organized by the counter-revolutionaries. But this was not done. Priests, and Catholics of all kinds, were immediately and directly attacked; from the very outset they were implacably hunted down, for no other reason than that of being what they were. They were executed on the spot, in cold blood, not in outbursts of sudden frenzy or mob excitement, but as the result of a hatred carefully and deliberately carried into action, of a conscious plan, inspired by systematic atheism, by the fanaticism of those who carry on war against God.

When the victims were questioned, or explanations were demanded of them, the matters treated were always religious, not political. The proofs that were sought were of the crimes of holding religious beliefs and indulging in religious practices. The examinations conducted or trials held, when there were any worthy of the name, always bore on these points. When laymen were arrested, one of the first questions asked them was if they were on good terms with their parish priest, or if they had friends and acquaintances who were priests or religious. Again and again, when the relatives of victims did their utmost to have them set free, one heard this terse reply:

"He's a Catholic, then? It will be difficult to save him."

The following incident is related of a well-known parish priest of Barcelona, Dr. José Vich. When he was arrested he did not reveal the fact that he was the parish priest of the Church of the Josepets. They asked him, suspiciously:

"Will you swear by your God that you are not the *cura* of the Josepets?"

He replied that, on the contrary, he was that person. He was hanged on a tree near Mataró and shot.

The facts of the case also provide a commentary from the theological standpoint, which have recently been developed by a competent writer, Canon Llovera.[1]

[1] "La Spagna e l'Educazione al Martirio." In *Rivista del Clero Italiano*, January, 1937.

It is common knowledge that in their strict definition of the word "martyr" theologians distinguish between the various attitudes which may be adopted by a Christian soul with respect to death for the Faith. There is self-martyrdom, of which many examples exist—as where a Christian has thrown himself into a river in order to save his honour. There is the case of a vocation which bears with it, if not the certainty, at least a high degree of probability, of martyrdom—as, for example, a vocation for missionary work in certain non-Christian countries. There is the free oblation of oneself for martyrdom which, in the heroic epochs of Church history, long since past, impelled Christians, here and there, to offer themselves to their persecutors and even to incite them to take action against them. There is the intimate desire and humble petition for the grace of martyrdom in order that thereby one may be united with the expiatory work of Jesus Christ. Finally, there is death in warfare against the enemies of the Faith.

All these various attitudes and acts of heroic virtue do not generally imply a duty of conscience for the Christian as such. Some demand particular motions of grace, or fall into the category of acts of *counsel*, not of *precept*. Others have not the character of martyrdom, and the free and impetuous performance of them may not always be laudable. In spite of the authoritative opinions of certain writers the practice of the Church confirms the criterion upheld unanimously by theologians, viz. that persons are not martyrs, nor may they be venerated as such, because they have fallen in war, even though fighting against enemies of the Faith, although this is in no way to deny the heroic, meritorious and laudable character of such deaths, suffered for the greatest of all causes.

For martyrdom, which consists in bearing suffering and death unjustly inflicted for the cause of the Faith, anterior acts of perfect virtue are not necessary. The general attitude of the Christian with respect to martyrdom should be the preparation of the soul for the acceptance of it should the case arise.

The reason for this is that martyrdom is not a product of specialized education within the code common to Christianity. Every case of education in the Christian code, with the never-failing pure and simple aids of grace, culminates in the opportune moment of martyrdom ; this consists in the sacrifice of one's own life, which is necessary and connatural in the order of grace, whenever the forces of evil are carried to the point of homicidal violence in order to destroy the good. Martyrdom is, in short, nothing but the highest expression, though the spontaneous expression, of charity.

When the right moment arrives (to quote the author already mentioned), the solid foundation of the Faith, which is the end in which the martyr is confirmed, the fervour of charity, which is the first and principal impelling motive of martyrdom, the impulse of courage, which is the elicitive habit of the immolation itself, all produce their connatural effect, and the act of the Christian martyr is complete.

These principles and distinctions should be borne in mind before one can decide which are the authentic cases of martyrdom among the heroic deaths figuring in narratives of any persecution of religion. It will at once be seen how many such cases there are in the history of the persecution in Spain.

An examination of the Spanish martyrology now in process of compilation will illustrate the doctrinal points expounded above. We find a general disposition on the part of the Christian soul—a collective state of conscience, it might even be said—for the experience of martyrdom, and the sense that the appropriate hour for martyrdom has come. We find also a wonderful manifestation of the potency of charity, making the Christian ready to endure any suffering, provided that by so doing he can pay due testimony to the faith which he professes, and pay it under the fiercest persecution. Objective statistics will doubtless show that the most splendid cases of martyrdom have been found not in Christians of a heroic and combative temper but in many others who were humbly following the road of spiritual development and exercise of the virtues with a profound faith, with an ample and generous charity and with a solid courage, showing their greatness not so much in the secondary act of meeting danger as in the principal act of bearing evils unjustly inflicted.

In the patience, heroism and gladness with which, for the sake of the Faith, they have borne afflictions, tortures and death, in the moving spirit of meekness with which they have forgiven their murderers and have prayed for them—in these resides the sublimity of our martyrs. There, too, is heard the characteristic note of their virtues—a supreme expression of love to God and to their neighbours. All this is clearly demonstrated by the martyrology of Spain.

CHAPTER XII

COMMENTARY ON THE DEFINITION OF THE POPE

As a final evocation of the glory of martyred Spain, and as a commentary on the pronouncements, already cited, of the Pope and the Bishops, let us add a few more to the innumerable examples of heroism and virtue called forth by the Spanish persecution, selected both from among the orders of the clergy and from the various classes of the laity.

The fury of the persecutors and torture-mongers against the Bishops has been unequalled. Venerable in age and dignity, they were from the first marked down as victims. As a general rule, their death was invested with something of a spectacular air by their murderers.

The Bishop of Guadix was led through the streets, grotesquely clad, to the accompaniment of a rain of insults. Finally, he was knifed to death and his body was burned. The Bishop of Sigüenza, stripped of his clothing and insulted by women of the vilest kind, was also subjected to public scorn. The Bishop of Cuenca had to suffer the most grievous form of martyrdom. The Bishop of Jaén was brutally murdered, together with his mother, a woman of eighty-four. He had taken refuge near Ciudad Real in a place known only to the authorities. Here, on August 22, 1936, he was found and cruelly tortured. His captors said, however, that they would defer his murder until he had witnessed the death of his secretary, whom it amused them to describe as his " son ". After he had seen the secretary shot he was thrown into the river, dragged out again and tortured once more until he died in the process, after pardoning and blessing his enemies. The aged Bishop of Almería was compelled to work in the trenches and subjected to indescribable cruelties. The Auxiliary Bishop of Tarragona led a life of great recollectedness in his prison ; and, as he was taken out to execution on a hillside near Montblanc, he gave his blessing to all whom he passed on the way. He was shot and his body was burned; when found, its right arm, which had been outstretched in blessing, was severed from the trunk.

Only two of the Bishops were given deaths which could be described as worthy of their rank and office—the Bishops of Lérida and Barbastro.

At the very outset of the Revolution the Bishop of Lérida was imprisoned with a considerable number of his parish priests and other well-known personalities, all practising Christians in the city. Among the company there was also a boy of sixteen. The revolutionaries took them all away in lorries, telling them they were going to Montjuich Castle, near Barcelona: instead of this they took them to the city cemetery. Finding themselves faced with the prospect of imminent death, the whole company of priests and laymen knelt around their Father and Chief Pastor and begged for his last benediction. The Bishop, who had been their comfort in prison, now became their strength. "Courage, children!" he cried, "within an hour we shall be in the presence of God." Then he began to recite the Creed, in which all joined as a supreme confession of their Faith, and gave them absolution. Before this they had each been made to dig his own grave; to the edges of these graves they were marched, and shot there, so that their bodies fell in and their executioners were saved the task of burial.

At Barbastro, the Bishop, together with sixty priests, religious and novices—chiefly Claretians—went from prison to execution chanting the *Te Deum*. It was a symbolic, almost a ritual procession, headed by the shepherd about to give his life for, and with, his sheep. When they were before the firing squad the Bishop blessed it with the words: "O Lord, forgive our enemies." The latter afterwards sang the International.[1]

Even those who escaped were pursued by the lust for extermination. In the prison-boat *Uruguay* a soldier was promised his life if he would go to Andorra with a gang of

[1] Ten Bishops in all were martyred. To the names given must be added that of the Bishop of Segorbe. The Apostolic Administrator of Orihuela, not of episcopal rank, was also murdered.

Anarchists in search of the Bishop of Solsona, who had taken refuge there.

Of the martyrdom not only of Bishops, but of priests and religious without number, incidents can be related remarkable for their testimony to heroic serenity and perfection of love.

The parish priest of Rubí, José Guardiet, was extremely popular throughout the diocese in which he worked.. He refused to escape when the Revolution came because he felt sure that no one would harm him, despite the fact that his village was of strongly left-wing sympathies. They arrested him, with two laymen, and were about to shoot all three when the laymen begged for a few moments' private conversation with him, which was granted. When they had finished, the priest told the militiamen that his two companions had just made their confessions to him and had charged him to say that they forgave them with all their hearts, as he also did, and that they would pray for them in Heaven. Six of the militiamen were so much moved by his words that they refused to fire, so the seventh killed all three.

The Archpriest of Mataró, José Samsó, was arrested with a number of laymen. His captors, who had been ordered to leave with a detachment of militiamen for the Aragon front, refused to go if they were not first allowed to shoot the prisoners. The local Revolutionary Committee, which was very moderately inclined (there have been hardly any assassinations in Mataró), opposed such a barbarous proceeding most vehemently. So the militiamen began to bargain : " Well, at least we must shoot the Archpriest."

When the Archpriest heard of this he offered to give his life if the rest were saved. They took him to the cemetery and ordered him to face the wall. Then he made signs that he wanted to address them and they allowed him to do so.

" You are blind," he said ; " to-morrow you will be sorry and ashamed for what you have done. But you are doing me no harm ; on the contrary, you are offering me the greatest blessing that I could ask for. I forgive you, I thank you and I assure you that I will pray for you."

As he finished, some of the militiamen flung down their arms but the rest were unmoved.

"Face to the wall," ordered the leader.

"Never," replied the Archpriest. "I will die facing my city and my church."

The parish priest of Ygollo, in the province of Santander, was an old man of seventy, who was in the habit of sharing everything he had with his flock. One night, when for some days he had been ill in bed, some militiamen from the village invaded his house and demanded that he should follow them.

"I am ill, very ill," he replied, "and I can't walk. You must do what you please with me."

In a moment they had shot him and left him in a pool of blood. A niece who lived with him came in and witnessed the terrible sight.

The old man had just sufficient strength to say to her :

"Did you see who they were ?"

"Yes," she replied.

"So did I," he answered, "and my conscience tells me that I never did them any wrong. Forget what has happened and forgive them as I have already forgiven them."

So saying, he died.

The following story is an excellent illustration of the meekness with which the Spanish clergy met their fate.

In the village of Tormellá, in the province of Gerona, there was a priest named Pedro Costa, an ardent and courageous soul, no more than thirty-five years of age. Whenever there had been anti-religious riots and demonstrations he would say to his companions :

"Personally, I would defend myself ; I would never yield to brute force."

When the Revolution broke out, however, he suddenly changed his mind.

"No, I shall not defend myself," he said, and threw away a pistol which he had in the house.

In due course they came to take him away. With a

splendid serenity and courage he kissed his mother and said :

" Don't be afraid, Mother. We shall meet in Heaven."

As they led him through the streets he said, with a radiant smile, to everyone he met : " We shall meet in Heaven."

They took him outside the village and burned him alive.

At Sitges, a seaside resort south of Barcelona, an octogenarian priest, who was very infirm, was taken from his house and shot a long way from the town. His last words were these :

" You can kill me, but you will never kill the Church."

The martyrology of the religious Orders has the same noble and sublime characteristics of which many notable examples have already been given.

Let us first recall a case which may well have been in the mind of the Pope when he spoke of the victims who " have gone so far in their generous heroism as to ask for a place in the vehicle along with those whom their executioner is taking to their death."

At Barbastro, between August 2 and 14, 1936, died some forty religious of the congregation of Missionaries of the Heart of Mary, founded by Blessed Antonio Claret. It became the usual thing for each group of them to sing hymns as they went from the prison to the place of their execution. The admiration caused by the radiant happiness of these martyrs was such that when one day a number of them were taken from prison and packed into a lorry which was to bear them to their deaths, a youth stepped in front of the lorry, and, when it stopped, asked that he too might be taken to die for his Faith.

Let us also refer to Canon Pedro Poveda, Archpriest of Burgo de Osma, founder of the Teresan Institute, a stronghold of the renaissance of Catholic pedagogy corresponding to the Free Teaching Institution,[1] which was the centre of

[1] [The Institución Libre de Enseñanza, as it is called in Spanish, was founded in the nineteenth century, by an anti-clerical educationist, Don Francisco Giner de los Ríos. From it have sprung many more modern secularist organizations, all of which regard Giner de los Ríos as their inspiration.—Tr.]

secularist education in Spain. One of the leaders of the latter institution had said, years before:

"On the day when we gain the victory one of the first to fall will be Father Poveda."

One can almost hear the rattling of the chariots going to the Roman amphitheatres as one relates the following story about a group of religious in Madrid. In their monastery four of the Fathers and a lay brother had been assassinated. The murderers packed the remainder of the monks on to an autocar and drove it over the body of the lay brother so that his companions should begin to realize the horror of what was coming to them.

Let us notice one significant characteristic of Catholic heroism which, if it was often respected in nuns, was a certain way to death with the men of the religious Orders. This is the steadfastness with which, for example, the Brothers of St. John of God, and the Hospitaller brothers in general, remained at their posts to care for the poor children, the aged and the mentally deranged among their patients. By performing this act of love while awaiting death they were quietly and perfectly fulfilling their daily task, the way in which the good Christian normally enters eternity.

As a last example of fortitude in the martyrs belonging to the religious Orders we may refer to the torture and death of the learned Capuchin Friar, Father Oriol de Barcelona, at Manresa. After being arrested and tortured, he was brought before the Revolutionary Committee, with his face bleeding and half-dead from exhaustion. His captors discussed what was to be done with him. They then took him outside the city and ordered him to blaspheme. Worn out as he was in body, his spirit was such that he replied by singing the *Te Deum*. Then he was shot.

No less admirable examples of heroism were given by the laity.

The following incident occurred in the cemetery of the Catalan town of Ripoll. Among those taken there for execution were Father Benito Juli, a Professor at the Seminary of Collell, in the province of Gerona, and his brother Rafael, an elementary schoolmaster in the same town, in whose house the Professor had taken refuge. One night, knowing that they were being watched and hearing that on the preceding day there had been several assassinations in the streets, they began to prepare themselves for the possibility of death. Early the next morning the house was invaded by a group of assassins. Don Rafael had six children, the eldest a girl of only seventeen, who clung to her father and refused to be separated from him. He exhorted her to behave like a good Christian, and not to fear death, since it was a great thing to die for Christ's sake. Only by her father's entreaties and the violence of the militiamen combined was the tragic separation effected. When the two brothers found themselves face to face with the firing-squad, Don Benito talked gently to them, explaining what was meant by the priesthood and what a mistake they were making in persecuting them. His last words were these :

" I am glad to shed my blood for Jesus Christ and I pardon you with all my heart. I ask you only one favour : spare my brother for the sake of his six children, who are entirely dependent on him."

" No," said Don Rafael, " I too have the strength to die for Jesus Christ's sake, and since He wills it so, I am not afraid of death."

His last words were : " Hail, Christ the King ! "

On the next day the eldest daughter went to the Revolutionary Committee with her brothers and sisters.

" Is it you who have killed our father and our uncle ? " she asked. " Well, we want to be shot, too, and to go to Heaven with them. When he bade us good-bye, my father said that those who died for God went straight to Heaven. So we want to die like our father and our uncle."

The revolutionaries said nothing, and sent them away.

On November 5, 1936, the Popular Tribunal of Gerona pronounced three death-sentences which were carried out a week later in the castle of San Julián de Ramis. The three victims were all fathers of families ; one of them, a municipal councillor and a leading Catholic, had been a great comfort to the other prisoners. When his sentence was communicated to him, his serene resignation gave place to an indescribable joy. His conversation, during the period which elapsed between the passing of the sentence and its execution, was nothing less than a commentary on the Beatitudes; his way of life was itself a prayer. On the night before he was shot he asked permission to take leave of his family and have supper with them in the prison. This was granted him. The emotion of that last meal and its effect upon the other persons may well be imagined. The condemned Catholic comforted his mother, and his wife, to whom a child was born two days after his execution, by telling them how happy he was to die for the cause of religion and how they must be glad because he was going to eternal happiness and that when the short separation of this life, so full of misery, was over, they would all meet again.

In the middle of this conversation, one of the children, a little boy of two, who, of course, understood nothing of what was taking place, tried to climb on to his father's knee and asked him to sing him one of his favourite songs. It was a terrible moment for them all. Summoning up all his courage, the father took the boy on his knee, kissed him passionately, danced him up and down, and to everyone's amazement, actually sang him the song he had asked for. Finally, he embraced each of his dear ones, and, as the prison door was about to be shut behind them, said with quiet courage: "Till we meet in Heaven." All these three victims told their executioners that they bore them no ill-will but forgave them freely and were shedding their blood gladly for the triumph of the Church and the salvation of their country.

None of our martyrs, it seems, failed to pardon his murderers. This is the characteristic trait of perfect charity, the most exquisite virtue of those who strive to imitate Our Lord.

When the Nationalists entered Barbastro, they made a significant discovery. In the building which had been used as a college by the Escolapian Fathers, all the priests and religious of the city and its suburbs had been incarcerated—Benedictines, Claretians, Brothers of San José de Calasanz:

about a hundred in all. On the walls of one of the large rooms in which they had been imprisoned, the following sentences had been traced in large, clear letters :

> " We forgive our enemies.
>
> " The blood of the martyrs is the seed of Christendom.
>
> " To those of you who are going to be our executioners, we express our forgiveness."[1]

Two further illustrations of the great spirituality of the martyrs may be quoted.

A young lawyer of twenty-two was assassinated at Valls, in front of his own house ; out of sheer cruelty, his murderers took him there from his prison to be executed. When his mother came out and saw her son's body in the charge of two militiamen, she knelt down, kissed his forehead and remained for a few moments kneeling in prayer. Then, with perfect naturalness and calm, she said these words :

> " You can speak no longer, son, so I will speak for you, for I knew all your innermost thoughts. 'Forgive my assassins, O Lord ; I pray with all my heart that, in return for having granted me the blessing of martyrdom, Thou wilt convert them to Thyself and make them to be with Thee in glory for all eternity.' "

At Badajoz, a doctor, Don Manuel Mesa, was assassinated by the Reds. When his murderers saw the Nationalist troops arriving, they said to his wife : " Now your avengers are coming." " No," she replied : " I want no vengeance, only forgiveness."[2]

What shall we say of the Christian youth of Spain ? Some of them are dying heroically on the battle-field ; others have won the honour of being martyrs and confessors in the midst of the persecution of religion. One of the most striking examples of their courage is a collective one. A great influence upon the development of youthful character was the Federation of Young Christians of Catalonia, known

[1] *Heraldo de Aragón*, March 30, 1938.
[2] *Al Servicio de la Patria*, Valladolid, 1936.

popularly as the F.J.C. In the dioceses of the ecclesiastical province of Tarragona, their numbers totalled 15,000. They were well organized, even in the rural districts, and their study circles, their acts of corporate devotion and the great Congresses which they held were models of their kind. Their co-operation in the work of Catholic Action heralded a new dawn for religion in Spain.

Down to the present, over three hundred of these young people have died in the course of the persecution; often they have been slaughtered in batches for the crime of having belonged to the F.J.C., which is recognized everywhere as standing for Catholicism in its most active form. Throughout their periods of imprisonment they have rejoiced at having been counted worthy to suffer for Christ's sake. Some monks, who had also undergone imprisonment, described to me the sensation of comfort and uplift which they derived from the arrival at their crowded prison of fifteen of these young people, all under twenty years of age. They came from the Bages district and they were all either working men or peasants. From the time of their original arrest, in their homes, they had been poorly treated, and they recounted their trying experiences with a surprising naturalness and lightness of heart. They soon infused a truly spiritual atmosphere into that place of affliction and dread. In their prayers, in their serenity, in the spirituality of their life lived in the face of an imminent death, they were the comfort, edification and inspiration of all.

Another group of twenty-four had just concluded a retreat when they were arrested with a priest from Montroig and brought before the firing-squad all together. The priest requested the executioners to wait for a moment while they made brief confessions and he gave them absolution. Then they all turned to the squad with radiant faces.

"Now we are ready," said the priest. "You can shoot."

One night a member of the Vich branch of the F.J.C. escaped over the fields and, as he was running along the main road between Vich and Roda, fell over a dead body. He stopped and examined his find and, looking around, discovered that it was one of fifteen bodies, all those of victims from his own branch of the F.J.C., who had been cruelly assassinated a few hours previously.

Another of the "Young Christians" was taken from his native village, Miralcamp, to Lérida prison, and there condemned to death. His grief-stricken mother was allowed to see him and to take leave of him on the night before his execution. Neither her tears nor her embraces shook his happy courage, and, as he kissed her passionately for the last time, he said:

> "Don't weep, Mother dear. Be glad with me: to-night will be the happiest night in my life. I shall love you still when I am in Heaven, and I shall await you there."

Some of the most impressive scenes took place in the prison-boat anchored in Tarragona harbour, against the clearness and blueness of that wonderful Mediterranean Sea. From the deck could be seen the executions which were being carried out only twenty to thirty yards away, on the shore. As each batch of victims was taken away the emotion of the farewells was contagious. The clergy who were there gave their blessing to those who were being led away to death, and, as they exchanged last embraces with their friends, one often heard the salutation: "Till we meet again in Heaven!"

One day the lot fell on a group of twenty young people, all members of the F.J.C. You would have thought they were going to some great *fiesta*. They went away to the strains of "Christ conquers, Christ reigns, Christ rules"; then they sang their federation hymn and finally all joined in the recitation of our majestic Creed. All this could be heard from the boat; and mingled with the reports of the rifles were heard voices witnessing to the glorious Faith. And so these young martyrs left this earth to unite their triumphant cries with the Hosannas of the blessed ones in glory.

We now reproduce three brief and splendid letters written by a youth who lived near Lérida who was sentenced to death with six companions. No commentary on them is possible: their spirituality speaks for itself.

To his former master and Spiritual Director :

" I write you these few lines. I have been condemned to death and in a few hours I shall be shot.

" I am quiet and happy. Soon I trust I shall be in glory. I renounce the pleasures of the world and the ties of worldly affection. I thank God that He is giving me such a death and such great hopes of salvation."

To two sisters and an aunt :

" They have just read me the death sentence. I have never been calmer than I am now. I know that to-night I shall be with Father and Mother in Heaven. I shall await you there. God in His Providence has been pleased to choose me as a victim of the errors and sins which we have committed. I go to death with great joy and tranquillity ; never have I had such great hope of salvation as at this moment.

" I have finished my mission in this life. I offer the sufferings of this hour to God.

" Whatever you do, don't grieve for me ; I ask no more than that. I am very happy. I only grieve at leaving you whom I love so much but I offer this affection to God, with all the ties that could hold me to this world."

Then follow a few words to each of the three in turn :

" Be brave, T——, don't weep for me. I am so intensely happy that I don't know how to thank God enough. I have been singing that hymn of ours : 'March on ; there's only one day's journey left !' It's so appropriate ! Forgive me for any trouble and sorrow I have ever caused you. I have always loved you so much. Now you understand : you are not to grieve for me.

" Poor little sister M——. You will be brave too and you won't let this pull you down. If you have any children kiss them from me : I shall love them in Heaven. Give my dear love to your husband : I know he will be a help to you and take my place.

" Dear Aunt : I feel so grateful to you just now for all you have done for us. A few years and we shall meet in Heaven. You will use those years, I know, in doing all sorts of kind deeds. This loving nephew of yours will pray for you in Heaven. Give my remembrances to —— and all my friends ; tell them that I die happy and that I shall remember them beyond the veil."

To his betrothed :

" Beloved Marion : Our lives came together and now God has seen fit to sunder them. With the greatest sincerity of which I am capable I offer Him all the love I have for you, love both intense and pure. It is for your grief that I mourn. Yet you ought to be proud, Marion dear : two of your brothers and your betrothed will have given their lives for God.

" Something very strange is happening to me. I can't feel sorry about my fate. A curious, powerful, intense inward joy comes over me. I want to write you a real good-bye letter, but I can't do it. I am just full of happy thoughts as though I were already near glory.

" I should like to tell you of my great love for you, of all the tender care I was keeping in store for you, of how happy we should have been together. But all that is a secondary matter. I have to take this great step now.

" One thing I do want to say, though : marry if you have the opportunity. And I will bless your marriage and your children in Heaven.

" I don't want you to weep : *you mustn't weep.* You must just be proud ; I love you. I have no time to write more."

Oh, holy, happy Christian youth of Spain !

Before concluding our narrativee let us relate a really beautiful and unusual story.

During the early days of the Revolution, not far from a church, the father of a family was arrested for having hidden in his house some articles used for Divine worship. He was taken for a priest ; but, after proving his identity, he was set free by the Committee before which he had had to appear.

In the middle of December 1936 he was travelling in a

motor-bus when an Anarchist militiaman recognized him and said:

"Now you shan't escape!"

Before long he found himself in one of the secret prisons of the Revolution, where he had to wait only a few hours before being taken out to execution. By a tragic coincidence, the prison was near the house where he lived with his large family; in fact, through the prison bars he could see his children at play. On the next day, one of the murderers was talking about him to a woman who lived near the prison and the victim's house, and she recognized him clearly from the man's description. "Do you know," she said, "that you have killed the father of a family of seven?"

"Good heavens, is that so?" exclaimed the militiaman. "I thought he was one of those priests."

When the widow of the victim, a lady of a truly Christian spirit, heard of her husband's death and learned the identity of the assassins, she called her children, the eldest of whom was a girl of only thirteen, and, when their first grief was over, exhorted them never to cherish any rancour against their father's murderers, reminding them that we are all the children of Our Lord who died upon the Cross, pleading for forgiveness for those who had been the cause of His death.

Three weeks later a friend, hoping to comfort her, told her that her husband's murderers had been killed in the fighting on the Aragon front.

"What a pity," she added, "that they didn't go there a month earlier!"

"No, you mustn't say that," exclaimed the widow, "for in that case my husband would not be a martyr."

And she made her children, who were there at the time, say a Paternoster for the assassins' souls.

Time would fail one to tell of the many testimonies of the deaths of the martyrs which are worthy of preservation, and of other humble Christians whose examples of love of God and their neighbour have produced such miracles of spirituality. Let us conclude by reproducing this last piece of evidence.

" One day, when I was visiting one of the innumerable devastated villages, I heard a phrase which I shall never be able to forget. The parish priest had been assassinated in front of the very altar at which he was praying, and a peasant was kneeling among the ruins of the church in the same place at which his priest had met his death. The peasant was praying with his arms extended in the form of a cross and I could not resist the temptation of asking him if he was praying for the victim's soul, He looked at me and shook his head :

" 'No,' he replied, 'we are both praying—he in Heaven and I here, for those who killed him, for " they knew not what they did." ' "[1]

What a simple, yet what a sublime expression of the Christian spirit to be found among our people ! What a marvellous vision of the intercessory and expiatory mission of the Church in Heaven and on earth, as it has been understood, and lived, by the faithful who have suffered under the persecution ! The Church, perpetually in prayer, kneeling quietly with its arms extended in the form of a Cross, forgiving, interceding and making reparation for all !

[1] *Nos Frères catholiques sous la Croix en Espagne*, p. 18.

EPILOGUE

WHEN Lenin, in far-away Russia, began to plan the invasion of Western Christendom, he thought first of Spain, which seemed to him the nation best prepared for complete Bolshevization. All the forces of Marxism, from social evolutionism to anarchism, have co-operated in the Muscovite attack on Spain ; the left-wing extremists overturned all social and political values and created an atmosphere of tyranny and civil war : liberalism in all its forms was either blind, or powerless to stop its devastating action.

One man alone had a sufficiently penetrating vision to oppose this advance while there was yet time. That man was Franco. But no one listened to him. While the Popular Front was at the height of its despotic power he was exiled to a lonely island. Before leaving, he did his duty as a patriot by describing to the President of the Republic the dangers with which Spain was becoming surrounded.

The President smiled and said to him : " Be easy in your mind, General. There will never be any Communism in Spain."

" All I know," replied the General, " and all I can answer for, is that there will never be any Communism where I am."

Franco has kept his word. Franco has been all over Spain ; he has been the inspiration, the brain and the arm of the Spanish rising and Communism has been defeated.

Stalin unleashed over Spain all the subversive forces at his command, resolved as he was to make Spain the strategic centre of the world revolution against the very foundations of civilized society in Europe.

Franco proclaimed his ideals—" God, Country, Civilization "—and, by means of a sacrifice unique in history, in a conflict unsurpassed for epic grandeur, Spain has achieved the triumph of humane and Christian ideals against a destructive and materialistic Sovietism. Franco has saved the Christian civilization of Europe from the most inhuman barbarism.

" We have to fight religion," declared Lenin. " Every Marxist is an enemy of religion." And Muscovite atheism, with its unexampled nihilism, has accomplished in Spain the most terrible religious persecution ever recorded in history.

" There are two universal forces in the world," said Lenin in August 1923: " the Catholic Church and Communism. Hence the inevitable conflict between them." The Red Leader of the Kremlin attempted to give battle to the White Leader of the Vatican. His arms are perversity, hate and destruction. Bolshevism, he said, means killing, burning and destroying whenever this will help the Revolution.

For the first time in history, said Pius XI, we are witnessing a cold, calculated and meticulously prepared campaign against all that is divine. And, confronted with so grave a peril to the Faith and to Christian civilization, Christendom has summoned its moral forces to save them. This it will not do by physical strength, nor by merely political and economic means, nor by the greatest and noblest earthly ideals, but by the potency and primacy of spiritual means, because it is from the most perverse spiritual principles that the monstrosities of Communism are born.

Communism can never be vanquished by political and military means alone; religion must arm both States and individual souls, in the spiritual and the social sense, for the defence and restoration of justice and righteousness in the nations. Catholicism is the one true obstacle to the triumph of Communism. And the *Præses caritatis*, to use the admirable phrase of the Church of Antioch, inspires and promotes the spiritual world-uprising by means of charity, which attracts and embraces all. " Never," cried Pius XI from his bed of sickness at Christmas 1937, " will we betray the tradition of love; and when a call comes to us, from however far, we will reply: ' We greet you in the name of Christ Who loves you.' "

In this great combat, to which the Pope is summoning the whole world, the first place belongs to Spain. She has taken arms to defend herself against the aggressor, who has used every means of aggression in an attempt to destroy the nation, body and soul, to quote Cardinal Gomá's exact definition of the nature of the Communist Revolution in Spain. Once the enemy is vanquished in battle, Spain will pursue the same great spiritual combat in times of peace.

Proudhon once ventured the prophetic remark that before long the world would find itself obliged to choose between the Church and revolution. It is said that Lenin, a short time before his death, remarked to a priest : " In a hundred years' time there will be only one form of government—our own—and only one religion—Catholicism. The force of your Church is a moral force, with no stain of oppression, and humanity needs both your force and mine."

Spain has made a definite choice for the Church and against the Revolution. In doing so she has made the world-victory of Communism impossible.

Franco is neither a conqueror nor a political dictator. Franco is the man who is leading a nation back to a total restoration, both of body and of soul ; these the Revolution attempted to destroy and these the Church will restore in their human and Christian plenitude. For the first time in contemporary history a nation is at war for ends which are not temporal : the Spanish War has been inspired by a deeply rooted desire for spiritual restoration. And the leader in this war is at the same time the Head of a new State which is by its own definition Christian.

On his investment with supreme authority Franco made the following declaration :

> " We desire only one thing, the greatness of Spain. For this to be attained there must be a union of all classes of society, a co-operation between capital and labour. And for this union to be established and maintained there must be one authority and one foundation—the Catholic religion."

" Our State ", he added later, " must be a Catholic State, both from the social and from the cultural standpoint, for the real Spain has always been, and will ever be, profoundly Catholic."

Seldom can a ruler have had before him such great possibilities and such ample horizons for the creation of a new State and the mission of directing and vivifying the energies of a people.

Never did a nation betake itself so ardently, so unanimously and so effusively to the restoration of its own nature and tradition in conformity with the ideals and standards of Catholicism, which is the soul of its historic culture and of its living patriotism.

In our day, for the first time, Church and State are uniting in a reborn society to create the necessary harmony and to work in co-operation with each other, so that the body and the soul of the nation may attain the perfect realization of their spiritual and temporal ideals.

All the anti-Catholic legislation of the Republic has now been repealed. Christian marriage is once more the social basis of the family ; Christian education is the soul and the atmosphere of the school. The Church is recognized and acknowledged as being a perfect society with all the plenitude of its rights. The " Charter of Labour " is the first Christian proclamation of social justice to be made by a modern State. The Catholic University will inspire the re-birth of culture. The future Concordat will be an effective guarantee of spiritual freedom and the renaissance of religion.

The foundations of this new Spain have already been watered with the blood of the Church ; and the Church will put all her energies into the construction of the edifice itself. She, the innocent and peace-loving, has been the principal victim of the Revolution. While Spain was fighting she was suffering and praying, tortured in her members by the fury of the Godless, and counting her martyrs and confessors by the thousand.

This is the choicest patrimony of the national renaissance, the glory of martyred Spain.

Before the Revolution the world was rather doubtful about the social and spiritual worth of the Spanish people. Their religion was spoken of as conventional, spectacular and sentimental. The quality of the hierarchy and the priesthood was not fully recognized; the work and activities of Catholic Action in Spain attracted little attention. But at the moment of decisive proof the hidden virtues of an intense faith have produced a florescence of heroism so sublime that it has amazed the world and vindicated for ever the Catholic tradition of Spain.

Now, to adapt the words of St Teresa, *nada turba, nada espanta:* there is no cause for anxiety or fear. The Proletarian Revolution, both in its spirit and in its works, is as good as vanquished. Our country will bring forth its fruits in righteousness and peace. God is showing us the royal road of future pacification, along which Spain will proceed to the providential realization of her noble destiny.

In the midst of the persecution, Spanish Christians have taken comfort in the thought of the Beatitudes of the Gospel. Blessed are the peacemakers. Blessed are the meek. Blessed are they that mourn. Blessed are the merciful. Blessed are they that suffer persecution for righteousness' sake.

The martyrs have suffered in meekness, have forgiven their enemies, and are effectually interceding for them still. Their example makes us hunger and thirst after righteousness: in the striking words of Paul Claudel, they have hastened the growth in our country of the reprisals of love.

During the persecution we have found that it is no light matter to profess the Christian faith. When peace is restored we shall have the chance to prove that we are not called Christians for nothing. In Balmes' words, we shall have to drown evil in an overwhelming flood of good. Hatred will be redeemed by love, the only force capable of uniting individuals and nations in creative activity. *Vis unitiva amor.* Only so shall we make victory fruitful.

We shall never forget the last cry of our martyrs: "Hail, Christ the King!" The Festival of Christ the King will henceforward be to us their festival. And the Christian constitution of the New Spanish State will be the witness of fidelity which it will bear to them, to the Church and to Jesus Christ.

The Bishops have placed the future of Spain under the protection of our martyrs. The Pope, who was the first to speak of their glory, was not slow to point out to us Spaniards that in their glorious footsteps we must follow, too. To those who had been faithful he gave this counsel as he blessed them. For those who had led or participated in the persecution of Christianity he had words of love and compassion.

> "We must love them, with a special love, full of compassion and mercy. We must pray that the serene vision of truth may return to their spirits and that their hearts may be opened anew to the desire and pursuit of true righteousness. We must pray that they may join us, when the rainbow of peace is seen in the fair sky of Spain, heralding a happy peace for that great and splendid country."

INDEX

The Mayflower Press, Plymouth. William Brendon & Son, Ltd.